T5-DHJ-805

When Can I Tell My Boss, "I Quit!"

Seven Lessons for Financial and Personal Rebirth in Retirement

Colin T. Nelson

iUniverse, Inc.
New York Lincoln Shanghai

When Can I Tell My Boss, "I Quit!"
Seven Lessons for Financial and Personal Rebirth in Retirement

Copyright © 2006 by Colin T. Nelson

All rights reserved. No part of this book may be used or reproduced by any means, graphic, electronic, or mechanical, including photocopying, recording, taping or by any information storage retrieval system without the written permission of the publisher except in the case of brief quotations embodied in critical articles and reviews.

iUniverse books may be ordered through booksellers or by contacting:

iUniverse
2021 Pine Lake Road, Suite 100
Lincoln, NE 68512
www.iuniverse.com
1-800-Authors (1-800-288-4677)

ISBN-13: 978-0-595-38362-7 (pbk)
ISBN-13: 978-0-595-82735-0 (ebk)
ISBN-10: 0-595-38362-9 (pbk)
ISBN-10: 0-595-82735-7 (ebk)

Printed in the United States of America

This book is dedicated to my beautiful wife,
Pamela.

Te amo, mi esposa hermosa!

Contents

Lesson Three: Learn to stretch and grow—both you and your money—while reducing losses

Stretching=growing. Change your internal "maps". Betting it all on one strategy. How to cushion losses to your money. Long Term Care insurance. Why Medicare and Social Security won't help.

Strategies to reduce losses while taking advantage of the upswings in the market

Monte Carlo analysis predicts if your money and resources will last.

Lesson Four: Learn to get your <u>money working harder</u> for you, rather than <u>you working harder</u> for your money.

The right use for Money Market funds. Sheltering severance pay from taxes. Roll-overs of retirement dollars save big dollars. Should you lease or buy a car? Advantages of a personal Asset Allocation model. Don't be too cautious early in your retirement.

Maximizing pension income. When should you take Social Security benefits and how to maximize them. IRAs—how much income can be withdrawn without running out of money. Immediate Annuities create income. Reverse Mortgages create income. Social Security benefits for divorced people.

Creative uses for life insurance. Selling your own life insurance policy for big dollars. Don't buy time-shares, cemetery plots, or anything similar. Should you pay-off your house before retirement?

Lesson Five: Learn to create new sources of income for yourself

Smart use of inherited money to create income. More income from annuities. Use your home to create a source of income.

The advantages of incorporating a business. Rental opportunities for extra income. "Last-chance" ways to create more income if you haven't saved enough!

Lesson Six: Learn to give from your assets and your life

Direct gifts of money to kids. Giving to children through Roth IRAs. Use of permanent life insurance to give to kids. Affordable strategies for saving for college. Coverdell Savings Accounts. U.S. Savings bonds. Are 529 College Savings Plans a good deal? Starting a small business.

Lesson Seven: Learn to live a life of fulfillment

Creative and meaningful work. Relationships. Controlling attitudes and feelings in the face of adversity. Are you afraid? Overcoming your fears. Creating your new life. Exercises to create a new life. Catalog your values and talents. Eliminate negative emotions. Choose to be an active creator of your life. Are setting goals worthwhile? Be prepared to change—again and again.

Acknowledgments

I wish to acknowledge my wife, Pam for her ideas, help, and support. She is a far better writer than I am. To Dr. E. Louis Mahigel, my guru in all things financial. To Stan Hustad, who encouraged me to start. To Dr. Mary Pruitt, who shared her writing experience with me. To Mike O'Rourke for his intelligent and generous advice. Finally, to my parents, gone now but not forgotten, for their love and support.

How the Story Began

"You can take this job and shove it!" sang Johnny Paycheck, in a popular country song a few years ago. It caught on with people who didn't even like country music, because he sang of something we've all wished for from time to time.

Having worked as a lawyer and financial advisor for thirty years, I'd counseled hundreds of people about retirement. They wondered when they could do it, hoping for sooner rather than later. Many were afraid they might run out of money. Some worried about how they were going to pay for medical costs. Of course, no one wanted to do anything risky, or to make a mistake, or to lose money. Clients puzzled over when to start taking Social Security. Others, never had "enough" and lived their whole lives with a "siege" mentality, trying to protect whatever they had from the "enemies" outside.

Through research and training, I learned the financial "rules" for my clients to follow that made sense and that worked. I educated them about these principles and encouraged people to apply the rules to their own situations. For the clients who saved, were disciplined, and smart about their choices, they had enough money for retirement.

In the past few years, however, I noticed something troubling. After my clients started retiring, they came to me as usual. But now they came for advice on spending their money. I realized that I didn't have much advice for them. Almost all the financial answers I had given was for people to prepare for retirement. There were very few resources for what to do with their money after they retired. I started a long program of studying this aspect of retirement. I discovered the "rules' were much, much different from those I recommended for pre-retirement. Economists call pre-retirement the "accumulation stage" and post retirement the "distribution stage".

Learning the rules for managing your money after retirement allows you to make decisions about when you'll retire and to prepare before you retire. That's because the "rules" are different for each phase.

There were few resources for my clients, so I decided to write a book to help them with their retirement decisions. I condensed all that I'd learned into the

Seven Lessons for Retirement

Lesson One: Learn to raise your financial IQ

Lesson Two: Learn what new problems you'll face and how to beat them

Lesson Three: Learn to stretch and grow—both you and your money—while reducing losses

Lesson Four: Learn to get your <u>money working harder</u> for you, rather than <u>you working harder for your money</u>

Lesson Five: Learn to create new sources of income for yourself

Lesson Six: Learn to give from your assets and your life

Lesson Seven: Learn to live a life of fulfillment

I wrote this book for four reasons:

1. To **warn** people of the problems they will face, financially, after they retire

2. To give people honest **strategies to succeed** with their financial issues and to overcome the problems they will face with their money.

3. To **encourage people to banish worry**. Instead, to stretch, to grow, to wrap their arms around change because it means new life and ultimately, freedom.

4. To remind people that **we all have something to give** to others. That service is the "rent we pay for living." That by giving, they can transform the second half of their lives into something greater than they imagined.

Instead of ways to save and invest money, now my clients began to question how to spend it. Would they spend it too quickly? What should they invest in to avoid risky situations? What would taxes do to their hard-earned savings? How could they get their assets working as hard as possible for themselves?

With these concerns in mind, when could they retire?

Lots of new questions with few answers to give them. As more clients retired, I realized that most people weren't getting much help with these questions. I could only find a handful of truthful and accurate books on the subject. Many columnists in magazines warned readers that the "rules" change once they retired, but didn't offer much advice. The most common advice I found were the bumper stickers that read: "I'm spending my children's inheritance!" Although there's a part of me that encourages clients to enjoy their money, this is hardly a responsible planning tool that gives people assurance and comfort.

Of course, my clients wanted solid, honest advice. Their questions worried them and caused them sleepless nights.

I was surprised at how grateful my clients were. Many of the things I learned had never been revealed to them. No one warned them of the different problems they would face and what solutions would work for these new difficulties.

If my clients needed and appreciated this information, why wouldn't other people? I started this book to fill that need.

Soon, the idea seemed too small to me.

Why limit it to strictly financial advice? I've always counseled my clients that money wasn't the main reason we got together. Money was only a tool to help them live productive, worry-free, and happy lives. Why shouldn't I continue that theme? It's a core belief of mine. In fact, after retiring, most financially secure people face deep questions of self-worth, purpose, productivity, use of time, anxiety, change, stagnation or growth.

It occurred to me that after retirement, many people have an opportunity they probably never had at any other time in their lives. Assuming they have enough money to not run-out, people in their retirement ages are the wisest, most knowledgeable, most experienced, toughest, gracious, and potentially the most giving people in our society. What wonderful things they could still accomplish.

Ironically, I didn't find many of my clients who were as excited as I was! Fear, worry, their present comfort, and weariness all held them back. Along with financial advice for these people, could I add something else to their retired lives?

At middle age, I'd tried something new that still makes me nervous. I started playing the saxophone and learning how to play jazz. For someone raised on the Beatles and the Beach Boys, this was strange and foreign to me. Not only the thought of playing the horn but getting up in front of an audience and performing, really made me sweat!

I'm not that special but after years of practice and work, I accomplished my dream and now, perform regularly in a jazz group. If I could overcome my concerns and grow, I was sure others could too.

This book will help you decide when to retire, to make good decisions about your money, and to live a rich life. In turn that will allow you to grow into the full person that you always wanted to be.

Lesson One:
Learn to raise your financial IQ

Lesson One:
Learn to raise your Financial IQ

Chapter One

Starting to think about retirement.
What do I need to know?

When I first met the couple, I was struck by how unorganized they were. Of course, many people who came to me for my financial advice were unprepared—that's why they came to me. But this couple was unique.

Charlie and Pat were in their late fifties and anxious to quit working. After working for years at a major corporation as a chemical engineer, Charlie wanted out. Pat had taught school for almost as many years. Their children had successfully "launched" from the home and completed college. This couple exuded health and energy. But they also exuded boxes of paperwork. They had the financial equivalent of the closet at home that never seemed to get cleaned out.

Pat had beautiful skin, large brown eyes, and a ready smile. She had kept trim and dressed in bright colors. Charlie, on the other hand, was short and tubby. Wisps of grey hair curled around his head. His ruddy complexion fit with the way he grinned, a slow curling of the mouth like a squirrel's tail. Both had a great sense of humor and seemed to have a good balance in their lives, between discipline and having fun.

We met for the first time, in my office, in the Spring.

Thanks to my wife, I kept my office spare. She'd taught me all about "feng shui" and the beauty of simplicity. I was stuck with darker walls, but tried to enliven things with green plants in various shades. I kept the lights low and preferred to meet my clients at an old, round table near the window.

After the usual chatter, we got down to business.

Charlie started, "Colin, we both want to quit working but have some concerns about all of this. It seems like such a big step, a huge change. After all, we've both worked for years, but our financial affairs are kind of a mess." He nodded and his wispy hair floated behind the movements. "We've got four concerns we'd like help with."

They were:

1. We want to get organized so that we know where our money is and what it's doing. Have we saved enough to be able to quit?

2. We don't want to make any big mistakes. We don't have a full lifetime left to correct them, so we don't want anything too risky.

3. We don't want to run out of money and become dependent on our kids. (At this point, both of them looked at each other and rolled their eyes.)

4. If possible, we want to leave something to our family and community.

I assured them they weren't the only "people in this boat", that the questions they had were very common. "I hear these all the time. There are hundreds of resources that can help you accumulate money to become rich and retire. Unfortunately, there aren't many resources for people to use after they retire."

"We're certainly not rich," said Pat. "Can we still retire?"

"That's exactly what we'll discover."

"You can help us with that?" she said.

"Sure. I've developed my **Seven Lessons for Retirement** that I'll teach you. They've worked for many others."

"Well, even lesson one would be helpful to us now," said Charlie. "When can we start?"

Charlie and Pat had some advantages others didn't. Charlie had a 401(K) that he'd put some money into for a long time. Pat had a teacher's pension through the state. They had lots of equity in their home and had some other retirement savings. Still, these resources were scattered all over the place. Neither one had a good idea of what they really had to rely on. Both were in good health, which led to one of their concerns. Unlike their grandparents, who had worked up until a few years before they died, this couple could live into their 90's, another 30+ years. Would their money last that long?

"Before we start looking at numbers, it's important to remember some larger issues," I told them. "Retirement's not so much about having enough money to last you, although that's critical. Rather, it's about independence, lack of worry, and a fulfilling life."

"Well…yeah," said Charlie. "We've made some rough estimates of our living expenses and what we anticipate our income in retirement to be. Seems to me, if the income is larger, we're okay. Right?" He looked to Pat for confirmation.

"That's a start. But before you even look at the numbers, think 'bigger'. Imagine you're at your funeral. How do you want people to remember you? Where do you want to go before you die? What kind of a life and person do you want to create? For most of us, our lives have been dictated by what other people and events made us do: teachers, bosses, parenting kids, clients and customers, phone mails, e-mails. Now, you're facing a wonderful opportunity to create your life in the way you always wanted to live it."

Pat nodded. "You mean to let our minds wander? Like, where do we live? What relationships do we want. How about our kids? What can we contribute to the world? Things like that?"

"Exactly. It's time to 'think big'."

"I don't know, Colin." Charlie's large stomach plumped up against the table. "It sounds kind of 'new age' to me. You know, the power of positive thinking. I've never thought much of that stuff. Most people never change at all."

"You're right. Most people never change. Change is one of the most difficult, scary things we face. Ninety-some percent of people don't do anything differently after retiring. That's okay for them. But for those adventurous few, acting on these larger questions is exciting and liberating."

"Will it really work?" Pat said. "What if I'm too old to learn new tricks?"

"Depends on what retirement will look like for you two. Will you quit at once or retire in stages? Actually, I've found that after all the celebrating is over, most people who quit working fall into a mild state of depression…usually because they haven't thought through the larger issues of what their lives are going to become. Money is the tool that enables you to create this new life you're looking at entering."

"Yeah," said Charlie. Can you help?"

"Sure. The cost for my help and other resources is relatively inexpensive. Let's work together. Alone, we often don't do as well. Here's an example."

A mutual fund research company named Dalbar, Inc. in Boston, studied people's earnings in the stock market. The found that from 1984 to 2004, the majority of investors earned an average annual total return of just 2.6% as compared to an S & P index fund that averaged, during the same period, 12% a year.

"That's hard to believe," Pat said. "Everyone at work always brags about how much they're making in their investments."

"Lots of bragging is like golf scores. Don't believe what you hear. Most people don't get help and they don't learn the fundamental lessons. Particularly, after they quit working, the rules are much different from what they hear on TV." I stood and offered each of them coffee or water. They chose water, so I retrieved three bottles of my favorite product from Costco: Perrier water.

Charlie unscrewed the cap, drank deeply, and pushed his chair back. "Those numbers make me very nervous."

But in the financial arena, knowledge banishes a lot of fear. Learning strategies to use will make this job easier. In fact, you'll come to realize that those people who don't follow any post retirement strategies are really the ones at the greatest risk. They don't know that, of course. If they knew of the wolves out there, ready to pounce and devour them, they wouldn't be able to sleep at night. By learning some of the new rules for retiring, you'll be able to make decisions about when you can quit. Some of these rules apply after you quit, but many of them are important to learn and apply before you retire. There's a window of time that passes quickly. You must take advantage of it, while you can. If you miss the opportunity, you'll face lots of difficulties in the future.

"Now that really makes me nervous!" said Pat.

The seven lessons will help you. In addition you have be willing to learn and change after you quit working. Regardless of how much money you have, your greatest asset will be your ability to learn new lessons and to act on them. This part is much harder than crunching the numbers. Because no matter how carefully you plan or how much money you have, circumstances will always change. Not only financial circumstances, but your own, of course. Tax laws, markets, demographics, and investment opportunities constantly change.

Charlie swept his hand across the table suddenly. "I don' know. The more you talk, Colin, the more you seem to bring up all the problems. That's not how I see our retirement. And, come to think of it, lots of people I know who've quit working don't worry about it much, either."

"That's probably because they've never been told what problems are lying out there for them. Since they haven't prepared or planned, they'll get hit the hardest, even if they don't realize it."

"How're we gonna handle all this?" Pat said.

"Don't worry. The lessons you learn will propel you through the challenges you're going to face. It'll be easy!" I assured them. "I call it 'raising your financial IQ'. Throughout all our lives, we've studied many things. For college courses, jobs, parenting, fixing the plumbing at home, and hobbies, for instance. Most of us are very good at the things we've studied…Well, I have to confess, that I'm rotten at home repairs. My wife won't allow me to use plug-in tools anymore."

Pat laughed with a knowledgeable chuckle.

The one topic most of us don't spend much time thinking about or planning for, is our financial situation. For most of us, it's kind of boring. We come to depend on the snippets we hear on TV or read in the Sunday business section of a newspaper. These are all helpful but really don't educate us, specifically, about our own situation. The first step for anyone, is raising their financial IQ's. Take the time to learn a few fundamentals that will help you for years. Particularly, after you quit working, the rules change considerably.

"What are these 'seven lessons' you keep talkin' about?" Pat said. "Is that part of raising our IQ's?"

"Sure. From my work in this area with hundreds of clients, I've developed seven, easy lessons that can be applied by anyone who quits working. They've been helpful for others and I don't see any reason they wouldn't help you, too." I pulled over a yellow pad from the edge of the table. Using a green, felt tip pen, I wrote out the lessons.

Lesson One: Learn to raise your Financial IQ

Lesson Two: Learn what new problems you'll face and how to beat them

Lesson Three: Learn to stretch and grow–both you and your money–while reducing losses

Lesson Four: Learn to get your <u>money working harder</u> for you, rather than <u>you working harder</u> for your money

Lesson Five: Learn to create new sources of income for yourself

Lesson Six: Learn to give from your assets and your life

Lesson Seven: Learn to live a life of fulfillment

I set down the pen and waited. I could tell from the way their faces twisted, they were interested but confused.

Charlie said, "These all look important for us to know." He paused. "Okay, I agree we should learn these new things. But Lesson Two intrigues me. What're the problems we'll face? When I've talked to the retirement counselor at my employer, she didn't say anything about problems. What're you going to show us?"

"We've been sitting a long time," I said. "Let's go for a walk outside. We'll go across the street to the park."

Pat and Charlie stood up. Charlie hitched his pants up over his generous stomach. When he let go, they fell back down.

Across the street from my brownstone office, a small city park encircled a lake. It was late enough in Spring that the park had started to turn green. Small snatches of ice resisted the warm sun, high in the southern sky. I buttoned by coat and led my two clients along the path that curved around the lake.

I knew of the large problems they would face when they chose to quit working. Some of those would come years later but they will come for sure. None of us can stop the problems but everyone can learn and prepare for them, to make sure they survive and succeed. It means making some changes, which most people resist. I looked at my clients. Would they be some of the smart ones and learn to change? Unfortunately, most of these problems are not considered or talked about before retirement. That makes their appearance later on, even more unsettling to people because they're unexpected. Most people simply accept their fate and shoulder the burdens as best they can. But, with knowledge, there is a way to succeed and overcome these problems.

We stepped around a series of puddles in the low-lying section of the path. Geese waddled around us and into the shallow lake, honking at our intrusion.

"Most people don't even know the problems will come and they certainly don't have a clue what to do about them," I continued.

Across the lake an older couple sat on a park bench. They had wrapped themselves in brightly colored ski jackets. The colors matched. The woman wore a knit ski cap, while the man had nothing on his head. Wind pulled his white hair up and away from his head. From hand to hand, they shared a bag of popcorn and threw some at the geese.

"They look retired," said Charlie.

"I've worked with hundreds like them," I said. "The first problem that comes up is having enough money. They all wonder if they'll be able to afford to quit working. Just like you. That's where we'll start."

Having been a compulsive note taker all my life, I made notes of our meeting.

What my notes said

1.   It's important to <u>learn</u> as much as you can about the issues and challenges of quitting work. Raising your financial IQ will teach you the strategies to survive and succeed.

2.   I developed Seven Lessons for Retirement that people could learn. The Lessons would enable anyone to prepare for the ups and downs of life after quitting.

3.   I also urge people not to limit their thinking and planning to money alone. For many, quitting work allows them to grow and change in wonderful, new ways. Smart use of their money will be the tool that enables them to lead a successful and fulfilling life in the decades ahead.

Lesson Two:
Learn what new problems you'll face and how to beat them

Lesson Two:
Learn what new problems you'll face and how to beat them

Chapter Two

Will we have enough money to live on and will it last long enough?

I explained to Charlie and Pat that this is the most common worry. Most people had a clear idea of their money needs for the first year or two after quitting, but then larger issues loomed: will Social Security go bankrupt? What about medical emergencies? Will we be able to afford to travel? How can we spend what we need and still leave something for the kids? Can we still go out to lunch? Play golf? They all revolved around the question of having enough money. Many people retired with large amounts in their 401(K)s. But when they faced the prospect of having to live off the money, those balances seemed to shrink like a puddle, drying in the spring sun.

I reminded my new clients to look at the long term. In the 1960's most people who retired at 65 died within five years. In fact, one of the reasons Social Security was pegged for a full benefit at age 65 was the knowledge in Congress that most people wouldn't live far beyond that age. It made Social Security very affordable for the government. There is an interesting story where the idea originated for choosing age 65. Otto Von Bismarck, the Chancellor of Germany in the early 1900's, picked that age when he set-up the first social security system in the world. It sounded like a great program for the German retirees. Unfortunately, the average life span at the time was only 47!

Today, statistics tell us that if you reach age 60, male or female, and you are in good health, you can expect to live into your mid-eighties. For women, it's even longer. For someone who started working at 22 and retired at 60, their money will have to last almost as long as they worked and saved. Often, people work part-time in retirement for that very reason. However, at some point, most of us get tired of working or are unable to work as much as we may need to. Plus, even part-time work will not add much to the nest egg. That means whatever a couple has at retirement is probably about the most they will ever have.

Pat reminded both of us that lots of her friends were depending on the equity in their homes to fund retirement, particularly since real estate values had sky-rocketed lately. But I cautioned them this wasn't solid. Real estate is a market just like the stock market and there have been big declines in value over the years. Bubbles can burst. The other problem, I said, is that equity's **locked into the house.** It's virtually impossible to get it out (you could mortgage the house, but then you have to make the monthly payments which will cut into your standard of living) until you sell and buy down or go into an assisted care facility.

Other people assume that, somehow, the government will take care of them. Besides Social Security, the government has never done this. There exists a minimal type of welfare, like Medicaid, for people but that requires the person to have exhausted almost all of their assets. Most of us wouldn't like the conditions required to qualify for this and, even worse, if you receive these types of benefits, you have very little choice left. The government will make the choices for the rest of your life for you. This is probably the last thing anyone thinking of quitting work, wants to accept.

A few are lucky enough to have pensions that automatically provide a steady stream of cash until death. Still, studies show that many of these are under funded, both public and private. When the Baby Boom generation retires and tries to collect, where will the funding come from? These pensions help, of course, but most of them don't take into account inflation—another obstacle I was about to bring up.

"This all sounds pretty grim," Charlie said.

"It'll be grim for many people. The first few years are usually okay. There's part time work, maybe severance pay, and life styles don't change much. Then, the expenses go up and worrying begins."

"How can we possibly prepare? How can we predict exactly how much income we will need for the next thirty years?" Pat asked. "Should we prepare a budget or something like that?"

"Well…" I answered. "For me…I hate 'em. They remind me of diets: they always make us give-up things, so most people go off of them eventually. They're negative. I suppose you could plan to cut your spending. All of us, to some degree, could do better. But let's face it, once you've enjoyed nicer things, it's hard to 'go backwards'. Realistically, most people don't do it. That idea doesn't work well."

"Could we sit down and calculate what our expected expenses will be?" Charlie wondered.

I explained that this is only accurate for a year or two into the future. Particularly for 30 years out, it's impossible to predict accurately what expenses are going to be. Many financial advisors use a percentage of present spending as a benchmark. For instance, some recommend planning on spending at least 70% of what you spend today. The theory is that many of your expenses will fall: you won't contribute to the 401K, or Social Security, or the union. You won't pay for commuting and parking. You may need fewer dress clothes. Other advisors caution that 70% is too low. You should plan on as much as 90% because even though some expenses are reduced, there are others that increase: you get involved in hobbies that cost money, you go out to lunch more often. You travel more. And, of course, inflation raises the prices of everything relentlessly over the years during retirement.

Why does it matter?

Because a 10% difference projected more than thirty years means the difference of hundreds of thousands of dollars. If you're short, that's not good. None of us want to start living on crackers and peanut butter for dinner every evening. Or even worse, none of us want to run out of money and have to depend on the government or our children and family.

I suggested Charlie and Pat consider a new Georgia State University study called "Benchmarking Retirement Income Needs" from 1988, which tracked retired people's spending habits. The study found that it all depended upon pre-retirement income. The higher the income, the higher the percentage to be replaced. For couples earning over $150,000 a year, they needed almost 90% of this amount in retirement. For couples earning less than $50,000, the figure was close to 70%. Personally, I liked the idea that someone outside of the financial industry had done this research. Over the years, I had heard endless advice from the media. After awhile, it all sounded re-cycled and confusing.

I told them to figure out yearly income immediately before retirement, multiply it by the appropriate percentage, and add 10%. Use this cushion as a "fudge" factor for unexpected expenses that aren't even imagined today. Later, in our lessons, we'd look at more accurate ways of calculating retirement income needs.

Will we be able to afford stamps?
Inflation

Charlie, Pat, and I walked to the north side of the small lake. We found a warm bench that faced south and sat down. A cloud of light green buds on the bushes surrounded us. The shade of green was different from that of summer. This was lighter, more delicate. Climbing higher in the sky, the sun melted the last of the dirty snow beneath the bench.

From the folder I brought, I pulled out two postage stamps. We all looked at them.

"The one on the left is from the mid-seventies. Notice it cost 15 cents. The other one, is the newest issue. It costs thirty-nine cents. When I warn people that inflation will be one of their worst enemies in retirement, they all nod in agreement." I paused as…they nodded in agreement. "But I know perfectly well, that most people don't get it."

"Can't the government do something?"

Charlie chuckled and his whole body wiggled. "I know the government's one of the reasons we have inflation. Our economy has had price increase, inflation, since the Revolution. Economists in the 30s and 40's concluded that a small amount of inflation was <u>good</u> for an economy. It kinda 'pushes' the economy, keeps it moving."

"Oh, sure," Pat interrupted. "I've also read that the government likes it because they can pay back their debts with cheaper dollars."

"Right," I said. "As the value of the dollar decreases with inflation, they become 'cheaper' so the government is really paying back less."

"Yeah but doesn't that really help retired people, too? Our mortgage payment is fixed for thirty years. Won't we get an advantage by paying smaller dollars twenty years from now?"

I agreed. "If…the retired person still has a house mortgage, but many people have paid them off by retirement. But debt payment's only a small consideration for retired people. The big problem will be the decreased <u>purchasing power</u> for everything else you need."

I pointed to the stamps.

It's very clear. In order to purchase a stamp today, it took almost three times the money as it did thirty years ago.

Here's the problem. Not only will someone who retires at 62 have to make sure their money won't run out in 30 years, they'll also have to develop a plan to **triple the income they receive now.** I stopped to let this bombshell sink in. While they were working, it wasn't too big a problem because most people receive cost of living raises or could move to higher paying jobs. After they quit working, these factors drop out.

I went on to share some devastating statistics about the effects of inflation. They were no longer dry numbers; they became uncomfortable:

Average long-term inflation: 3.1%

Inflation reduced purchasing power by:

>—51% in the decade of the 70's

>—39% in the decade of the 80's

>—25% in the decade of the 90's

At 3.1% inflation, purchasing power decreases by:

>—11% in five years

>—23% in ten years

>—40% in twenty years.

Department of Labor studies show that the average life expectancy is 78.5 years. For educated, healthy people—much longer. Second, surviving spouses may easily live from 83 to 97!! The study also noted that medical care costs increased by an average of 44% during retirement and are heading much higher.

For instance, if a couple had a family income of $80,000 at the start of retirement, at 3.1% inflation, in fifteen years they would need an income of $126.465 just to stay even and just to maintain their present lifestyle.

In the park, I took a deep breath and looked up into the trees. A large oak spread over the edge of the lake. At this time of the year, the black branches were easily visible. They twisted like old arthritic fingers. Green points of color dotted their limbs.

I thought back to an incident with my grandparents in the 1970's, a time of high inflation. We were sitting in their kitchen at the Formica table, my grandmother having just served doughnuts. I told the story to Pat and Charlie.

My grandfather had sold fruits and vegetables during the Depression so they were particularly attentive to the produce prices at the store. I remember them, in their retirement, complaining about the cost of bananas, peaches, and lettuce. "Can you believe the price of steak?" my grandfather said. He threw one leg over the other. At his age, the bell-bottoms he wore made me laugh to myself.

"Steak? I can't even make a decent salad anymore," grandma said. "And gas. The cost of gas! I used to be able to fill my tank for six dollars!"

They went on to name other products and services that had risen in cost. As the months went by, my grandparents were beginning to be priced out of some of these things. Home heating costs rose to the point they became cautious about taking the driving trip to Florida again. Because even though they could turn down the heat while gone, they still had to pay all the other higher costs: insurance, property taxes, and the heat. It was almost like watching an emphysema patient taking smaller, labored breaths each month. The rising costs choked-off many of the activities and dreams my grandparents had hoped for twenty years earlier when they retired.

Most people know what inflation is, of course, but while they're working, they usually get pay raises, cost of living raises, or new jobs that pay more. The true impact in the loss of purchasing power doesn't affect people much. But these inflation protections don't always continue after quitting work. Suddenly, people on fixed incomes start to feel squeezed because of what the cost of daily items has risen to. The sad fact is that most people don't have any plan to triple their income as they live the long years of their retirement. And it may get even worse as live spans continue to stretch into the future, further stretching people's small resources.

We all stood up. A yellow cloud shivered in the tree behind us, as a flock of finches became nervous. We hurried away and they settled back on the branches in the warm sun. We shuffled back to my office, reluctant to leave the outdoors.

The avalanche of coming taxes!

"I've got clients in their mid-seventies who are paying more in taxes than they earned in salaries ten years earlier," I told them when we were back at the conference table.

"That's unbelievable!" Pat said. "I thought taxes went down during retirement."

Charlie added, "Everything written and the advice I've always heard is to delay paying taxes until you retire. For years, I was told to max-out my 401(K) contributions and deferred compensation plans. The idea was during retirement, when I wasn't working, my income would drop. With less income, taxes would drop, too." His pink skin still flushed from the walk outdoors. "What you're saying runs counter to everything I heard."

I shrugged. "Yeah. But I told you, the rules have changed. New strategies are needed for the time after you quit working."

I also pointed out the political realities that retired people will face in the next ten or more years. Along with those recently retired, an estimated 75 million baby boomers are scheduled to retire also. They will control trillions of dollars of assets. This represents the largest, wealthiest group ever, in the history of the country.

Most analysts and economists feel this pot of money will be tantalizing and available for government needs. There will be constant pressure from government to tap into these assets in a variety of ways. Inroads have already been made.

"Who knows what the future holds?" I said. "If the government gets hungry, this is the first place they'll look to grab some tax revenue."

"So what can we do? What're these taxes you're warning us about?" said Pat.

The good news is that there are easy, legal ways to minimize this avalanche of taxes that are coming your way. Some of these strategies can be used <u>before</u> you quit working.

Everything will be taxed!

1. <u>All pension income</u>—401(K)'s, deferred compensation, IRA's, Tax Sheltered Annuities, 403(b)'s, defined benefit pension income, and defined contribution money <u>will be 100% fully taxable.</u>

This was the "deal" we all made with the government, whether we realized the ramifications or not. Every dollar, that we contributed to our retirement plans, meant we could deduct a dollar from our earned income in order to reduce our income taxes as we worked and contributed. If a person put $10,000 a year into their 401(K), they could deduct $10,000 from any other income they earned during the same year. Along with the interest they paid on their home mortgages, for most of us, this was the biggest deduction anyone of us took to our advantage. People didn't think about twenty or forty years later. The accountants all told people not to worry…the tax dollars deferred were worth it. "Max-out the pension plans," they said.

People have to pay taxes during retirement. So what?

The government rules worked like water through a garden hose. What went into one end, had to come out, eventually, from the other end. If people deducted their contributions at the front end, they had to pay taxes on the money they took out at the back end, at retirement. The rules said they couldn't touch retirement money without paying a penalty until they reached 59 ½. After that, they could take out whatever they wanted but they would have to pay full income tax on every penny, as if they were working at a job. Even if they died and there was still money left in an IRA, for instance, children who inherited the IRA would also have to pay full income tax on withdrawals. There is no way to avoid paying the tax.

That was the "deal" we made. But what was so bad about that?

By itself, a full tax on money coming out of retirement plans wouldn't be so bad. It was the fact that the government forced people to take money out of their retirement plans, whether the person needed or wanted the money. They're called the **Required Minimum Distribution,** or RMD rules. They mandate that when a person turns 70 ½ (I never have figured out why the ½ year is always used…?) the government has a forced distribution schedule that everyone must follow. It says that you have to take a certain amount of money out of your retirement plans each year. And it continues each year whether you need or want the money. You don't have to spend it but you must take it out and, of course, pay full tax on it.

By itself, that's not too bad.

I showed Pat and Charlie an example of two clients I was working with.

The husband was 72 this year and the wife just turned 70. They had carefully saved a lot during their working years—which was good but had put almost all their savings into the husband's 401(K)—which now gave them big problems. Even though they had "rolled-over" the balance in the 401(K) to a self-directed IRA, they still faced a big tax bill. (A rollover is a tax-free exchange of dollars from one type of retirement account to another type.) It is almost <u>always</u> a great idea to use the rollover IRA, I told them and promised to explain why later.

I showed them the couple's situation:

Value of IRA @ husband's age 71	$700,000
Required Minimum Distribution factor	26.5%

To calculate, they divided $700,000 by 26.5%, which gives the number of dollars the husband must take out of his IRA for the year, declare it as income, and pay taxes on= **$26,415**.

This year, at age 72, here's what happened:

Value @ 71	$700,000
Less distribution last year	- 26,415
	673,585

Remember, the IRA will continue to grow (hopefully!) during the year. It grew at 7%, to increase by $47,150.

Value at end of year	$673,585
Growth during the year	+ 47,150
New value	720,735

Now, the husband must divide this new value by the RMD factor (which goes down 1% per year) He must divide $720,735 by the new factor of 25.6%= **$28,153** dollars that he must take out and declare as taxable income. It's easily possible that the value of the IRA will grow faster than the distributions, meaning that this couple will have to take out larger amounts every year and pay larger taxes every year.

This process goes on every year until the husband dies. If the wife had her own IRA, she too, would have to go through this same process starting at 70 ½ and will then add her income to her husband's, possibly pushing them both into a higher tax bracket.

What to do?

I explained that taxes would <u>have</u> to be paid one way or another, at some time. For instance, by contributing less to the 401(K) while working, a person will pay more tax on their income now but less tax in the future. It really becomes a question of timing.

"But if I contribute less to my 401(K)," Pat asked, "I won't have saved enough for retirement."

"Nope. I'm not suggesting you save less. Instead, invest the same amount in different places."

"Like where? A Roth IRA? Would that make a difference?"

What's a Roth IRA?

Good choice. A Roth IRA is a 'reverse' of a 401(K) in some ways: contributions today are not deductible from your income but when you take money out, after 59 ½, it's never taxed. Therefore, the RMD doesn't apply.

I went back to my two clients' example.

If the husband had $400,000 in a self-directed IRA and $300,000 in a Roth IRA, set-up before he retired, not only would his RMD be cut almost in half but he and his wife may remain in a lower tax bracket. They'd have less income subject to taxes and, possibly, those taxes would be in a lower bracket. They'd receive the same income but may cut their tax bill by 50%—simply because of where they put their money.

If there's an employer matching program—typically up to 5% of the employee's salary—contribute up to that amount but not a penny over it. Up to the full match you automatically receive a 100% growth rate! Free money. Beyond that, you may face an avalanche of taxes when you hit 70 ½. The younger the employee, the more important this strategy becomes.

The tax on the tax–Social Security benefits taxed

"By itself, the RMD can be bothersome, but when you add it to your Social Security benefits, then it gets much harder," I said and noticed their scowls. What could be worse? they seemed to ask.

"You know that in the 80's when the Social Security system threatened to run out of money, the government made major changes?"

"Sure. Like I can't collect my full benefit until age 66 instead of 65," replied Pat.

"That's right but it's only one of the things they did. They raised the amount we have to contribute in taxes from our salaries. They raised the maximum income level that Social Security taxes would be calculated upon. And, for folks in retirement, the worst thing they did was to <u>tax the benefits that they have paid for, from their payroll taxes</u> which they paid while working."

A tax on the taxes already paid?

I showed them an article from the Wall Street Journal, dated July 18, 2001. More people are paying taxes on their Social Security benefits. A record 9.6 million individual tax returns for 1999 reported taxable Social Security benefits. That was up from about 6% from the prior year, the IRS says.

The problem of paying taxes on benefits for which you already paid lots of taxes is no longer a problem for the rich. Remember that FICA taxes are paid with after-tax income. You can't deduct your Social Security taxes from your earned income.

"I can't imagine we'd ever have to pay taxes on Social Security," Charlie protested. "We're not poor but we're certainly not rich. It can't apply to us"

When do Social Security benefits become taxable?

I showed them the figures. They weren't pretty:

The government created a category called "Provisional Social Security Income." It means that at certain income levels, a portion of your Social Security income benefit will be taxed at a portion of either 50% or 85%.

Provisional Social Security Income

Single Taxpayer			Married Taxpayer
$25,000	up to	————————	$32,000
		50% taxable	
$34,000	up to	————————	$44,000
		85% taxable	

When the income is added up from the previous couple:

Income from IRA distributions	$28,153
Wages (wife worked part-time)	6,000
Social Security benefits	20,000

Provisional income is $28,153+ $6,000+ $10,000 = $44,153, so Social Security is 85% taxable.

Adjusted Gross Income	$28,153
Wages	6,000
85% of $20,000	<u>17,000</u>
Income subject to income taxes	$51,153

Pat and Charlie looked at the figures for a long time. It didn't seem fair, they told me.

My response make them look up. "You're beginning to see the **compounding effect** of all these tax problems. The RMD for instance, by itself, creates big problems but when you add in the Social Security tax, it really becomes an avalanche of taxes. Add to this rising property taxes which you pay on your home, even after you retire, and you can see why some of my clients are pulling their hair out."

"What can we do?"

"That's why we're meeting. So I can teach you the lessons to minimize these problems. Do nothing. The avalanche will bury you." I turned back to the papers on the table. "Let's use my clients as a place to start. We've already seen that while you're working, you should not contribute too much to your 401(K), Deferred Comp, SEP, and any other 'qualified retirement plans.' We saw that the wife was still working part-time while the husband collected his Social Security. Two ideas:"

1.   **Don't start to collect Social Security** until both spouses have stopped working.

2.   If one continues to work, like the wife here, she should **establish an IRA** (or use her employer's plan) and contribute some of her income to the plan to reduce her taxable income.

By now, we were tired from all the information from the financial lessons. I sensed they'd reached their saturation point. "Enough for today?"

Pat sighed, ""How'd you guess? I know it's important and you make it simple to understand. Still that's the problem. I understand these things now and I'm worried."

"Sure," I said. "That'll motivate you to learn to avoid these problems. You'll also learn about some wonderful opportunities that you can take advantage of… it's a lot more fun! Believe me! We'll pick up here next week."

What my notes said

1. People worry they'll not have enough money to live on if they retired. How could they know when it is okay to quit working? Would their money last?

2. People could use my Seven Lessons in order to answer these questions. University studies have calculated what percentage of a person's present spending should be anticipated for spending in retirement.

3. I warned about inflation and used the example of the cost of postage stamps. People need to prepare to **triple** their income in the next thirty years, just to stay even with their life style now.

4. My clients learned about the Avalanche of Taxes that were headed their way. Particularly, when all the future taxes are added, it will take a huge bite out of retirement income.

5. Finally, I warned them about the tax they'd have to pay on their Social Security benefits. Up to 85% of the benefits could be taxed.

6. I tried to encourage my clients because there are ways to beat these problems that aren't hard to learn or do.

Chapter Three

Becoming educated about the money challenges

Pat and Charlie met me at a Caribou Coffee near the office. We found a larger table in the corner away from most of the customers. We ordered the daily coffee while Charlie ordered a large latte.

"I get 'em to make it with 2% milk or even whole if they've got it." He patted his round stomach and said, "S'pose I don't need this stuff, but what the heck! Life's short, as these guys here say. They sure taste great!"

We moved over to our table. Charlie blew gently on the hot foam, sniffed it, sipped it, and drank finally. He looked up and his cherubic face broke into a grin. "Let's get going!" he said.

"What's the lesson for today?" Pat said.

"Well, it's a review to some degree. Remember when we talked about the 'avalanche of taxes' coming?"

"Yeah, how can we forget it?" Charlie said. "You're gonna give us all the secret ways to avoid them?"

"No, you can't avoid them, but you can minimize 'em. And that's better than most people will do. I've got some good ideas for you."

Pat said. "Since our first meeting, I've told some of my friends about all these taxes and you know what?" She looked from one of us to the other. "First of all, everyone's really shocked. But then, they act like there's nothing they can do about it! I can't figure that out."

It's a common problem. Most people are worried to some degree, but they avoid the issue, as if it'll go away or something. It's the same psychology that has driven down the savings rate in this county to zero. Everyone knows they're going to need more money in retirement, but nobody's saving. Why? Most people have no idea how bad this tax situation will be and, as a result, they're not prepared for it. It's going to be a huge shock for many.

"Why aren't they prepared?"

"Nobody's telling them. And although I'm not the smartest guy in the world, anyone could hire me to teach them what we're going to cover today. People think they can do this on their own," I said. "Here's the example I use. Do you change your own oil in your car?"

"No…too much trouble. It's easier and they take care of everything." Charlie set down his latte. "I see. I'm willing to pay someone about a 100% fee to change my oil, but hesitate in paying for good financial advice."

People in the media keep complaining that financial advisors charge one, two percent for their advice. I know I'm biased, but it seems like a good deal to me. For the small cost of an expert, you can save thousands of dollars and maybe even earn thousands too. Other resources are companies like Fidelity Investments, one of the largest and best financial services company in the country. Find them at their website at www.fidelity.com. They have a variety of free services for retirement planning, tax avoidance, and general education. In addition to online resources, it's a good idea to work with an experienced person, if nothing else, to give you a "second opinion". What you're really paying for, is experience and most important, judgment.

"We're here to learn," Pat said. "So let's get to the lesson."

"Remember when I taught you that almost every source of income you'll get in retirement will be taxed?"

"Yup."

"Pension income, 401(K), deferred compensation, 403(b) income, probably even your Social Security benefits will be taxed. That's because of the 'deal' we made with the government. While working and contributing, we took a tax deduction. Now, when we want the money back, we have to pay a tax on what we take out."

"There was that 'compounding effect' you talked about. Where the taxes on pension income are added to taxes on Social Security, and then when we got to a certain age, we had to start taking money out of our IRA's…which is also taxed on top of everything else."

"That's the Required Minimum Distribution rule that kicks in at age 70 ½. Good memory. You may be interested in seeing this." I pulled out a chart of the factors for the RMD. I traced along the side with my finger. "See? If you're 70, you have to divide the balance in your IRA by 27.4%. That tells you how much money you have to take out for that year and pay tax on. So, let's say you got $300,000 in your IRA. On the year you hit 70 ½, you <u>must</u> take out $10,949."

LIFETIME REQUIRED MINIMUM DISTRIBUTIONS

Age	Distribution Period	Age	Distribution Period	Age	Distribution Period	Age	Distribution Period
70	..... 27.4	82	..... 17.1	94	...... 9.1	106	...... 4.2
71	..... 26.5	83	..... 16.3	95	...... 8.6	107	...... 3.9
72	..... 25.6	84	..... 15.5	96	...... 8.1	108	...... 3.7
73	..... 24.7	85	..... 14.8	97	...... 7.6	109	...... 3.4
74	..... 23.8	86	..... 14.1	98	...... 7.1	110	...... 3.1
75	..... 22.9	87	..... 13.4	99	...... 6.7	111	...... 2.9
76	..... 22.0	88	..... 12.7	100	...... 6.3	112	...... 2.6
77	..... 21.2	89	..... 12.0	101	...... 5.9	113	...... 2.4
78	..... 20.3	90	..... 11.4	102	...... 5.5	114	...... 2.1
79	..... 19.5	91	...... 10.8	103	...... 5.2	115 &	
80	..... 18.7	92	...... 10.2	104	...... 4.9	Over	...... 1.9
81	..... 17.9	93	...... 9.6	105	...... 4.5		

Application: Used in calculating lifetime required minimum distributions from IRAs, qualified plans, and TSAs. For example, assume an individual turned age 74 in 2005, and on the previous December 31, 2004, his account balance was $325,000. Using this table, his life expectancy is 23.8 years. He must receive a distribution of $13,655 ($325,000/23.8 = $13,655) for the 2005 year, no later than December 31, 2005. Use of this table is required for 2003 and later. See also, IRA distribution planning.

Source: Treasury Reg. §1.40(a)(9)-9, A-2

"We don't have any choice in this?" Charlie asked.

"Nope. But there are ways to minimize this problem."

"Oh yeah. You advised us to stop maxing-out 401(K)'s and instead, put the money into Roth IRA's, for instance."

"Right. But what about the money we already have in IRA's, 401(K)'s and so on?" Pat said.

There are a number of strategies that can be used. It depends on what assets you've got. For instance, if you've got permanent life insurance. (Permanent means you never lose coverage for your entire life, as opposed to term policies.) These policies provide an alternative place to put "retirement" funds. That's because once the money is invested into mutual funds within the policy, they grow tax deferred and may be "borrowed" from the policy without paying income taxes on the amount borrowed. I told Charlie and Pat we'd spend a lot more time looking at these great options.

Invest in Municipal Bonds

This is an old idea that's used often. People invest in municipal bonds, issued by local governments either by buying the bonds themselves or mutual funds that invest in these types of bonds. The key is, they're free of federal income tax. And if you buy one issued by the state you live in, they could also be free of state income tax too.

"I've got a friend at the company who's been buying these for years. Most of his retirement money is in bonds," Charlie said.

The tax-free aspect is great but there are a lot of drawbacks.

1. You're very limited in choices to buy. Governments only issue so many of these things. Especially, if you buy from the state where you live. An alternative is to invest in municipal bond mutual funds.

2. Rates of return on these are generally low because they're very secure and tax-free. Sometimes, it's hard to keep up with inflation because of the low rates paid on these bonds.

3. If you're really following an asset allocation model, you can only hold a certain percentage of your assets in these types of fixed-income vehicles.

"So they have a place but it's pretty limited," Pat said.

Remember another big problem. If you've got these in a retirement account, they grow tax-deferred anyway. So it's like wearing two raincoats. You get the tax benefits of the IRA and the municipal bonds. You don't need both. It's only when you take out income from them that they pay off well. Here's another idea.

Tax-efficient investing:
buy growth stocks with dividends

Charlie pushed his empty cup away and became animated again. His eyebrows rose and fell and he talked faster. "So, you're suggesting investing in things out-side of our 401(K)'s?"

The idea is like the 401(K) strategy, in that you don't max-out your possible contribution but instead, invest in things like this. You can buy good, growth stocks outside your retirement plans and hold them. You don't pay any tax until you sell them. And then, you only pay long term capital gains tax, which is much lower than your income tax rates. If you die and haven't sold the stock, your heirs get the stock at the price it sold for when you died…meaning they don't have any gain to report for tax purposes. You may also get some additional income from the dividends.

Charlie said, "What's the downside?"

It's hard to find a good stock, a single company, that'll grow consistently year after year. And again, you're violating your asset allocation model because you've got a lot on money not only in one type of investment but in one stock. You're extremely undiversified. But like all these ideas, it works for some people. With any strategy, there's never a perfect solution. All of them have their benefits but it depends on the person and their situation.

How can a person get diversification?

For the average couple, it takes a lot of money to be as diversified as a group of mutual funds. Then, you've got the job of selecting which stocks you're going to invest in, and watching them. It's possible, but why not make it easier and just invest in a group of mutual funds where the managers do the work for you? The fund will invest in dozens of stocks of good companies for you, giving you diversification even though you may not have thousands of dollars.

"That brings up a question I meant to ask you," Pat said. "I've read that the majority of mutual fund managers can't outperform the market. If that's true, why would you buy managed mutual funds and pay the extra fees. Why wouldn't I just load-up on index funds? Wouldn't they just track the movement of the market?"

Lots of columnists in the media talk about this. Statistically, they're right, that most fund managers can't beat the indexes for growth rates. But as usual, there's more to this than you read. For one thing, an index fund is okay, but it's only as good as the stocks that managers put into it. You can look at the Standard and Poor 500 market index, composed of 500 stocks, but there aren't any index mutual funds with 500 stocks inside of them. So, I wonder how accurate are some of the index funds? And, the index funds tend to have a higher "beta".

"What?" Charlie said.

Beta is a measure of how risky they are. What research has shown, is that in down markets, the index funds tend to do worse than actively managed funds. And remember, that how far your funds drop in a down market is as important, maybe even more important, than how high they go up.

"Oh yeah, the time and the percentage gain it takes to get back to where you started," said Pat.

"Right. The other thing to remember is the whole point of diversification is to have a balanced group of funds that, taken <u>together</u>, should beat the market. If you look at only one fund and manager, they're not going to beat the market all the time."

We remained silent for a while. Charlie finally stood and bounced up and down. I could tell he was really excited.

I said, "All this emphasis on growth rates, beating the market, and so on **shouldn't** be the focus of a retired person. But I know the media always writes about this. Let me tell you a story."

Suppose you want to go on a trip, but you're not sure where. There are several cars you could choose to get you there. Car One can go up to 85 mph but has a tendency to break down sometimes. Car Two goes 65 mph but is more reliable. Which one would you choose? This is what all the media talks about—the speed of the two cars. Which fund will outperform the other? The question I want answered first is, where am I going? Once I decide I'm going to Chicago, it may not make any difference which car I take because my main goal is <u>to get to my destination.</u> What difference does it make how fast? That's what I try to get my clients to look at. Where do they want to end up in retirement? If 65 mph will get them there as well as 85 mph who cares which car they take? In many ways, maybe Car Two at 65, with less risk, is actually better for them.

"So it's a whole different perspective?" Pat said.

I said, "Of course we want our investments to do as well as they possible can. But this constant focus on performance takes our attention away from what's really important."

"That's why you've forced us to look at where we want to end up in retirement and then, work backwards to see how we can get there? One good thing about your perspective is that it's a lot less worry. I've got friends who want to retire but when the market drops a little, they're afraid to quit working until the market's up again." Charlie said.

"You've told me not to worry too much about the ups and downs of the market so long as we're still on track to reach our retirement goals," Pat said. "That's made my life a lot easier."

"Somebody smarter than I said it: keep your eyes on the prize," I said.

The door to the coffee shop opened to the outside. Several customers came in at once and held the door open. Suddenly, warm air puffed in, scented with lilacs and sun. It seemed to revive us all.

"What about Roth's?" Pat said. "You've talked a lot about them. Can they help us reduce costs?"

Reduce Costs with Roth Conversions

I kept smelling the warm air. I suggested that we go outside to the tables set up in front of the window. They both followed me. Puffballs of clouds sailed across the bright blue sky. When the clouds passed, heavy sunshine fell on us.

Roth IRAs were named after the U.S. Senator who pushed for their creation. They are retirement vehicles just like regular IRAs. The difference is that you contribute money to the Roth after you've paid tax on the dollars so you don't get a tax deduction in the year of contribution, like you would to a 401(K), for instance. The other side of the coin is that when you take money out of them, later, you never pay any tax on any withdrawals. After five years, you can take out the original money you invested and after 59 ½, you can take out anything from them without penalty or tax. These are one of the few tax-free investments that are readily available to all of us.

There are a couple more guidelines:

1. You had to have some earned income from a job of at least as much as you contribute

2. Your Adjusted Gross Income cannot exceed $95,000 for singles and $150,000 for married couples, otherwise you can't use a Roth

3. The maximum contribution per year per person is $4,000 although this number will go up in the future

Once past the review, I started to teach them about a "Roth conversion".

"This is really a process that you go through only at the appropriate time," I said. "I'll give you some tips when this works the best. Let's look at my clients Harry and Sally."

Harry is a 63 year old retired engineer from a software company and Sally, who's also 63, ran her own business as a temp employment service. They're happily married and looking forward to their new lives. Here's what they've got:

Harry's 401(K)	$600,000
Sally's SEP retirement plan	400,000

Remember the avalanche of taxes coming to these two unsuspecting people: at 66 both will start taking Social Security which will give them an income of about $40,000. Sally also has a Navy pension for the years she served that will give them an added $27,000 a year for a total income of $67,000. At 70 ½, each of them will have to start taking money out of their retirement plans because of the Required Minimum Distribution rules.

Charlie thought for a moment, then said, "And everything will be fully taxed."

"You're so bright, Charlie," I laughed. "Yeah, they're gonna get killed! Remember: you have to pay the taxes but there is a way to minimize them." On the napkin before them, I used the green pen to draw.

401(K) ----------------> IRA -----------------> Roth IRA

"That's the 'process' you mentioned?" Pat said.

"Yup. The strategy is to 'roll-over' Harry's 401(K) money into a self-directed regular IRA."

Pat interrupted. "I get it! There aren't any taxes or penalties charged to roll-over the money to the IRA."

"Nope. The next step is to move the money from the IRA to a Roth IRA."

"Tax-free again?" she said.

"Nope, again. Since Harry got a deduction on his tax return years ago when he contributed to the 401(K), he has to pay full tax to move it to the Roth IRA."

"So what's the point?" Pat said. "Taxes are taxes, aren't they?"

"Nope. Let's suppose they wait until they're 70 ½. Harry's $600,000 could grow to more than a million. Which would you rather pay taxes on: $600,000 or $1.2 million?"

Charlie raised his hand in my face. He flushed to a mild pink. "Wait a minute. But you don't pay tax on a $1.2 million lump of cash. You pay it over the rest of your life, a little each year as you draw it out of your 401(K)."

I nodded slowly and waited.

Pat interrupted, "So in five years, even though he takes money out and pays taxes on that amount, the rest of his 401(K)'s still growing. Five years later, it might be worth $1.5 million and he has to take out even more and pay taxes."

There are some strategies that help even more.

1. Spread-out the withdrawals from the regular IRA over many years to minimize yearly taxes

2. Take a withdrawal after a big drop in the market so the value of the funds are down and fewer taxes are due

3. Take the spread-out withdrawals during a time when neither person is working, so they aren't bringing in more money–you want a low income year

4. Start the Roth IRA at least five years earlier to fit in the guidelines

5. Take a withdrawal if you have a high deduction year

6. Delay taking Social Security benefits until the withdrawals are all done

With Harry and Sally, both had started small Roth IRA's years earlier. At 63, they quit working, rolled-over each retirement plan to regular IRAs. Then, they started withdrawing money over a four-year period and moving it into their Roth IRAs. They started receiving the Social Security benefits at age 66, which pushed-up their income the last year of a withdrawal but they managed to save thousands of dollars in taxes over the rest of their lives.

"You know, there's another benefit here," Pat said. "With their money in the Roths, the government no longer has control over when and how they use their money, since there's no Required Minimum Distribution rule for Roths. So, they get complete control over their own money and how they're gonna use it."

"Good point," Charlie said. "You know, I've never heard anyone talk about this. I can't think of one retired person who's thought through this."

"Once you understand the lesson, it's easy. Trouble is, if the couple is past seventy years of age, this still works but not nearly as well as if they had started this in their 50's or 60's."

"And I can see how we'd save thousands of dollars. It seems odd to pay the taxes now," Pat said, "since everyone's always advising us to delay paying taxes as long as possible."

"That's the hardest part of my job. It hurts people to pay the taxes today, even though they may understand how much more, they'll pay tomorrow. It's the same old thing of people putting-off painful decisions. But you can clearly see, in the long run, why it's smart to pay some of the taxes earlier."

A light breeze blew the napkin off the table. I retrieved it and asked Charlie if I should consider bronzing it for posterity. After all, someday my ideas could be very famous when they became well known.

Cutting Costs with Permanent Life Insurance

I relaxed in the warmth. Charlie leaned back in his chair.

A permanent life insurance policy provides another strategy that works to cut the cost of taxes. Permanent life insurance works like a Roth IRA. Money invested in the policy is not tax deductible but it grows tax-deferred inside the policy. It's a tax free withdrawal if you take out money by "borrowing" from yourself.

"Then would you use the same process that you used for the IRA to Roth IRA?" Pat said.

"Right. You can substitute the life insurance policy for the Roth IRA. It works the same way."

"That doesn't mean we should start a new life insurance policy, does it?" she asked.

"Probably not a good idea at your age. It gets very expensive. Later, we'll talk about when it may be worth it to pay for insurance but in this situation, I don't think it's a good idea. Many people have permanent policies they invested in years ago. For most people I work with, those policies are just sitting there, growing at very low rates like 2%–3%. They don't know what a powerful tool they have!"

"Why couldn't I just move money, a little at a time, out of my 401(K) into my life insurance policy? Do I still need to funnel it through a regular IRA?" Charlie said.

"Yes. Remember we learned a few weeks ago that you should roll-over your retirement money after you quit the job. There are those administrative costs, the inflexibility of many retirement plans like 457 deferred compensation plans, and so on. You still want to get away from those problems. The roll-over to an IRA solves those. Now, you're faced with the taxes and the life insurance policy is a place to park your money until you need it."

"We're back to insurance products, again," said Pat.

They're very flexible and can be used in a variety of ways. There are also annuities, which are giant IOU's with an insurance company. You invest money with them and later, you are able to get it back, with some growth in your money. Within the annuity, you can invest in mutual funds or fixed income vehicles. Some annuities even offer guaranteed returns—something like a CD would guarantee. In the meantime, your money grows tax-deferred and when you take it out, only the growth portion is taxed.

"So if we had an annuity, we could use that like a Roth IRA, too?" Pat said.

"Yeah. It doesn't give you all the advantages of a Roth or life insurance but it works better than paying all those taxes."

"I don't know," said Charlie. "I read lots of articles about what a rip-off they are and that insurance companies just sell 'em to charge high fees. And if the fees are high, that means my growth is low."

"You're right. There are some companies out there who rip-off the public. I don't work with any of them but they're out there. But all of them probably charge more fees than a Roth, let's say. We come back to one of the problems with the financial media…they're generic in their advice."

"It applies to everyone, not necessarily to me and my particular situation."

"Right. I don't think there are many financial products that are all bad. Rather, different products are for different situations. Sometimes they make sense, sometimes they don't. I don't sell a lot of annuities, but for some people's problems they're the perfect solution. Do you know about left brain/right brain decisions?" I looked at them to see if they remembered. "Psychologists tell us that the left brain controls the logical, analytical decisions we make while the right brain is the intuitive, emotional decision maker. People make decisions for all kinds of reasons. In the end, I have to respect that. I've got some clients who would never touch an annuity and then, there are others who swear by them and use them extensively. The wonderful part of the financial industry today, is the large number of products we can choose from. The number of resources available and the cost of them has never been better for the consumer."

Pensions, Social Security benefits, Military pensions etc.

When do you start taking a pension? When do you start taking Social Social Security benefits? For reducing taxes, remember, we've been learning that you want to keep your income as low as you can while you're converting the money to a Roth. Or, if you have some high deduction years, you can absorb a little more income and still keep your tax rate lower."

"Most of the people I work with are looking forward to starting Social Security at 62. Is that a good idea?" Pat said.

"Like I said, each couple's a different situation. We'll learn more about that next time. Can you hold with that question?"

Health Care Costs!

In the early eighties, 70% of early retirees had employer-paid health care coverage. It would last for the rest of their lives. By 2005, only 27% of firms paid for this kind of a benefit. Today's baby boomers are in for another shock.

"Another one," Pat groaned. "I'm done getting shocked by all of this!"

Some more interesting statistics from the US Department of Labor.

In 1992, employers required retirees to pay about 39% of the cost of health care coverage. In 2002, that figure had risen to 68% In 2002, 17% of all large employers required retirees to pay 100% of health care costs.

Add to this the fact that Medicare is trying hard to reduce its costs by paying the doctors and hospitals less. Some doctors have stopped taking Medicare patients.

This is why. People would be surprised to know that research found that Medicare pays only about half of all the bills for most participants.

"It's a nice day…no more bad news," Charlie pleaded.

"I'm just warming you up. The news is full of this and I know I'm not telling you anything you don't know. Costs of health care are going up and the number of people demanding/needing the care is going up as the baby boomers grow older."

"And the trend for dealing with this is to shove the extra cost on the individual?" Pat said.

"Right. It's going to happen more and more. But once you understand this, you can look for ways to minimize the effects. And, as usual, if you do your research early, before you retire, you can probably do pretty well."

"Kinda like your strategy on taxes?" said Charlie. "You can't eliminate 'em completely but you can keep them as low as possible."

"Right. There are two stages to these health care problems."

The Bridge Years

Most of us will qualify for Medicare health coverage at 65. Like my two clients, for those who leave the sheltering arms of an employer with a health plan, they've got to cover the years in between, the Bridge Years. Here are some ideas.

1. The first step is to contact your present employer. Under federal law, employers with 20 or more employees are required to offer medical expense coverage to retirees for up to 18 months. (COBRA) The retiree pays all the cost of the insurance but it's usually a good deal because you get the benefit of a group plan with its lower costs. It buys you time to find another strategy or turn 65.

2. Your present employer may offer health coverage after retirement on a continuing basis. This is rare but some companies still do it.

3. You should check on professional organizations, unions, fraternal groups. They offer group plans to their members, usually at reduced costs

4. Veterans are eligible for many benefits also

5. If you're looking at private policies outside of group coverage, shop around. The costs vary widely

6. Start your own business. You may be able to join with other businesses in a group policy and your premiums could be tax-deductible as a business expense

7. Whatever policy you choose, raise your deductibles and co-pays. You are really self-insuring for the routine expenses and passing on the costs of large or catastrophic losses to the insurance company. Premiums can be cut tremendously this way. Be sure to have a cash reserve in place to pay the deductibles if you need to

8. Work part-time with an employer that will cover you under their group policy

"Then when we hit 65, we're home free?" Charlie said.

I winced. "Uh...not exactly. Let's look at your choices after 65."

After 65 Years

The best choice, if you can get it, is to try and get a health plan from your former employer or union. Sometimes, they're integrated with Medicare, but they usually are better than Medicare alone and offer good prices for premiums. When these aren't available, most people choose Medicare. Part A pays for hospital stays and Part B for doctors and non-hospital care. You pay a premium for Part B and it's been going up each year. In addition, there are deductibles and co-pays.

1. Since the costs are rising, most people, about 85%, buy a Medicare supplement policy. (Medigap) Because Medicare only pays about half of all expenses, these policies fill-in the "gap" and come with a variety of coverages and varying premium cost. (Ten types available)

2. Medigap insurance is purchased from private insurance companies so shop around. It's a good idea to check the history of the company's premiums to see how much they've been rising in the past.

3. One of the biggest costs is for drugs. There are a couple ways to reduce these costs, too.

    a. Join a drug purchasing plan. These private groups try to get large-scale discounts on popular medications. Check carefully, however, because sometimes, the discounts are not worth the costs and efforts. (Research has shown that on the average, people only save about 10%—better then nothing)

    b. Medicare prescription drug coverage. Effective in 2006, Medicare participants will be able to sign up for a Medicare drug plan or join a private health plan that offers drug coverage. You will have to pay another premium with annual deductibles. After the deductible is paid, the government will pay 75% of the first $2,000 of drug costs until the total expenses for the year reach $2,250. From that level to $3,600 the participant pays everything and above that, the government will pay 95% of the costs. (Very complicated)

4. Health Savings Accounts are available for people retiring less than 65. It's a tax-free savings account established by your employer. You can contribute pretax dollars to it, let it grow tax free, and take out money for medical expenses tax free. It works something like a Roth IRA except instead of retirement expenses, these are to by used only for medical

expenses. The best strategy here is to let the money in the HAS grow as long as possible.

5.   There's a good web site at www.medicare.gov for more, accurate information

"Whew! What a mess," Pat said. "I never knew it'd get this complicated. But you're right: at least I can see a strategy to work through this. It's possible."

Get out of jail free card–will I ever get our of debt?

It's hard to overestimate the high cost of debt. Lots of debt is very expensive. Credit card debt, for instance, could go as high as 29%+ per year. Car loans, though cheaper, still carry hefty percentages. Then, there are the retail stores' debt. It's common for a retailer to run a sale and then extend their own credit to the buyer instead of using a major credit card. Or they offer no payments for 12 months that lead to very high rates if you fail to completely pay off the balance in 12 months.

First of all, if you find yourselves not paying more than the minimum every month, you have too much debt. Or if you go from card to card without paying-off the previous ones, you have too much debt. If the balance creeps up month to month, you're in too deep.

Debt had some interesting issues:

1.   If people have enough income to support high levels of debt, it still may not be good.

2.   High levels of debt are a drag on retirement income, particularly if you're drawing from IRA's, pensions, Roth's, etc. because you can't always "give yourself a raise" by taking more out of those retirement accounts to cover more debt payments

3.   Obviously, the high cost of debt robs dollars from your pocket and costs you a lot in useless interest

4.   Don't forget the "opportunity cost" which means the cost of spending your dollars for debt payments when they could've been used instead, for something more productive. You lose the "opportunity" to invest or spend that money.

5.   Is all debt bad? No. As I had taught them weeks earlier, the debt on a house was usually a "good" kind of debt to have. Or if you borrowed to

make an investment like a new business that produced an income for you, debt and the "leverage" it provided were very good

The true cost of debt is, therefore, much higher than people think. It has to do with the "opportunity" cost of money. I showed them an example.

Interest rate charged on a typical credit card	18%
Add to that the lost opportunity cost that you could've earned with the same money invested in something else	<u>10%</u>
True "cost" of your debt	28%!!

Of course, that means with a $10,000 balance on a credit card, the person will "lose" almost $3,000 in a year. Shocking, when people first see the example.

Like many people, my clients paid down their bills but a balance always seemed to remain no matter how hard they tried to eliminate it completely. I showed a technique to them that worked for many others.

First, you have to "find" some extra money. That means squeezing out $50, $100, or more each month, depending on what you can. Use this additional amount to add to your regular payments. This helps to "jump-start" the process.

There were many ways to accomplish this. Usually, it meant searching through a monthly spending pattern to see if any expenses could be cut. You could raise the deductibles on your home and auto insurance from $250 to $1,000. Then, save some extra money in an emergency fund to cover the $1,000 if it's needed due to an accident. That will cut your insurance costs quite a bit and free-up some extra cash you could devote to pay more on debt. For anyone who's been victim of the "latte factor" by spending a lot of money on expensive coffee drinks and treats during the day, you could still find ways to cut some of those expenses. You could begin by taking your own, healthier lunches to work Eat out fewer times each month. Each family is different and could find extra money in different places.

Once you "find" $300 a month extra, (or whatever amount you can) you are ready to plug in the numbers.

Start by making a list of each creditor. You can leave out your home mortgage because there are reasons that you shouldn't pay off that. Next, list the balance owed and, next to that, the monthly payment. Divide the balance by the payment. For instance, if you owe $20,548 to the Credit Union for car loans and the payments were $600 a month, write that down Then, divide 20,548 by 600, to get the result of 34.2. Each divisor you calculate for each debt, tells you what priority to assign to that debt. The lowest divisor gets the first priority.

Some experts tell people to pay off the highest interest debt first. But this system, gives priority to the lowest divisor debt. Next, take the present payment, $600, and add the "found" money to the payment, giving us $900 a month. When you divide $20,548 by $900 you will get the number of months that it will take to pay off this debt. The number is 22.8 months.

It's possible, using this system, that debt can be paid off in three years! Of course, that means during those three years, a person couldn't take on more debt. If they did, the whole process would have to be started over again.

"That's the biggest problem with this," I said. "People just can't seem to stop charging things long enough to get out of debt!"

"Do you recommend that retired people be debt free?" Pat said.

"Not necessarily. It depends on each situation. Let me give you an example. Pat, remember the student loan you used for your master's degree?"

She answered, "Yeah, I think the interest rate is less than 3%."

"Remember inflation is running almost 3% now and may go higher according to some economists. That means your fixed payment will never change but the value of your dollars decrease by 3% a year."

"The upshot is I'm getting 'free' money!"

"Right. You're using other people's money, the bank's in this case, for free. That's the kind of debt I wouldn't pay off. Beside, I'm already helping you get 'free' money."

"Oh?"

"Think about your 401(K). Over the years you've put in, let's say, $300,000 and now it's worth more than $600,000 and in a few years it could easily grow to $800,000. Where did the extra $500,000 come from." I looked from one to the other. "Did you 'work' for that?"

"Well…when you put it that way. I never thought of it like that," Pat said.

"It's kinda like getting on a train. You pay a little for your ticket and the train starts out very slowly. You even wonder how it's going to pull all that weight. But in time, it gets going and soon, it's roaring along. You didn't do anything but put a little money into your ticket and get on board."

"Are there other debt reduction plans?" Charlie said.

"Oh, of course. They're hundreds probably. This is one I like. I guess whatever plan works for you is good. I know there are lots of financial advisors that say if you have a high income in retirement you can afford to carry more debt. I'm from an old school. I don't like debt. It almost always means that I'm taking money from myself and paying it to others to make them rich, rather than me. Still, the issue of debt is probably the one, greatest reason people can't get ahead. It's a psychological issue for many people. Shopping and buying are so intrinsic to their lives, they can't cut back. It also means their freedom to quit work will be delayed, maybe for years, because of so much debt."

The sun slanted lower over the billowing trees outside the coffee shop. I think we were all tired from this lesson. We pushed back our chairs and stood to stretch.

"I'm sorry to have to go over all this stuff. I'm the first to admit it's tough."

"But essential. Don't worry. You've always taught us that even a little work on these issues makes a world of difference," Pat said. She raised her head until she caught my eyes. "But promise me, the next lesson will be more fun?"

"Of course, of course! That's the point: to make this more fun than work."

What my notes said

1.   I introduced the lesson with a reminder of all the taxes we'd pay in retirement but I promised to give them several strategies to minimize the taxes.

2.   These strategies include:

–Buying municipal bonds or municipal bond funds

–Investing in growth stocks and holding them for the long term

–Roth IRA conversions to save on taxes in the future

–The use of permanent life insurance, which works like a Roth IRA, to reduce taxes

3.   I taught them ways to deal with the high costs of health care after they retired.

–During the "bridge years"

–The after-65 years, with Medicare

4.   I suggested a way to help them get our of debt before they retired, which will make the decision to quit working easier because they have freedom from debt and the drag it would put on their retirement income and life style.

Chapter Four

Strategies to beat the problems

A few weeks later, we were back in my office.

Pat said. "You make me worry that we'll never be ready to retire or never stop working."

"That's why we're having lessons. Knowledge will set you free. We talked about the four main financial problems people face in retirement. There are other challenges, of course, but these seem to affect everyone I work with. Remember them?"I paused, then said, "Will you have enough money to last? Watch out for the effects of inflation. Avoid the avalanche of taxes. And what should we do about Social Security."

"It seems overwhelming," said Charlie. "All the questions and choices. I remember, as a child, going into McDonald's. At that time, there were only two choices for burgers: plain and with cheese. Three types of malt and one size of fries. It was limited but simple. Now, I go into McD's and it takes me a half-hour just to read the menu, let alone choose something!"

I laughed. "Yeah, I remember that, too. What I'm trying to do with the Seven Lessons, is to simplify the whole process for you. I educate you on the problems, provide solutions that work, and then you can make the decisions easily. Most advice focuses on ways to accumulate enough money to retire. I focus on ways to succeed and protect yourself after retirement. Today, I want to show you a variety of strategies and tools that you can use. Some may be specifically helpful for you now. Others will be helpful in the future. Most important, I want you to learn the choices."

Delay using your retirement money and saved assets

When trying to answer the question whether you'll have enough money to last for your entire lives, strategies like this are very obvious. You could continue to work part time so that you delayed tapping into your assets. Statistics show that almost 50% of retired people are working at something for pay. Besides the additional income, working has many other benefits. People need the social aspects of a workplace. Some need a "reason to get up" in the morning. Structure in their lives. Medical science has shown recently, that continued challenging of the mind and learning promote better mental and physical health.

Also, a delay in taking benefits from a pension or Social Security would help. Usually, by delaying these payments, the benefits increase, often just in time when people need higher incomes to maintain their purchasing power. In addition, many pension plans increase the benefits by 30%–50% if you are able to wait to collect them. And, as we've seen, if you are in the process of using Roth IRA conversions, it's best to keep your income as low as possible. Delay in taking Social Security benefits or pension benefits, helps to keep your income low during those conversion years.

Get your money working harder for you

Commonly, when people retire, they don't add much to their investments. Then, the money has to start working, instead of the person. Unfortunately, most people work harder than their money works. It should be the other way around, with their money working for them. People don't take advantage of safe, easy ways to make their money work hard in order to keep it growing well into their retirement years. They need to move their money into better places for better growth. Some of this requires a simple act of learning and paying attention to where their money is at any given time. You must re-evaluate these things regularly.

Roth IRA's give you one of the best breaks

Don't forget the Roth IRA. It's a 'reverse' of a 401(K) in some ways: contributions today are <u>not</u> deductible from your income but when you take money out after 59 ½, it's <u>never taxed.</u> Therefore, the Required Minimum Distribution (RMD) doesn't apply.

If you had half of your money in a 401(K) and half in a Roth, your RMD would be cut by almost half and you'd also fall into a lower tax bracket. You could receive the same income—from everything in a 401K) for instance—but cut your tax bill by maybe as much as 50%. This is a result of simply putting your money in a different place.

If your employer has a 401(K) matching program—typically up to 5% of the employee's salary—contribute up to that amount but not a penny over it. Up to the full match you automatically receive a 100% growth rate! Free money. Beyond that, you may face the avalanche of taxes when you reach 70 ½.

In addition, there are many investments that the government will never touch. Primarily, these are insurance-related products. They represent a huge industry with lots of money, which equals lots of political strength. Many of their products have enjoyed tax advantages for dozens of years. So, we hope they will continue to have many tax breaks for the average person.

"But we don't need life insurance," Pat said, "do we?"

Probably not. Primarily, when kids are grown, the need for insurance decreases. Remember what the goal is: avoid the taxes you'll have to pay. There are two, main insurance investments that can help. One is life insurance and the other are annuities.

I pulled off a piece of paper from a yellow pad, smoothed it on the table before us, and retrieved a green pen. I wrote the words in bold letters.

The many advantages of life insurance

"First, you have to understand I'm talking about permanent insurance," I said.

"Is that called 'whole life'?" Charlie asked.

"Used to be. What I'm talking about is called 'Variable Universal Life' insurance. This is another fancy word the industry uses. Here's how it works."

I drew a picture of a large, green cloth bag. Into the top, I poured the premiums an investor would make. From the bottom a faucet drew-off the cost of the insurance, which was less than the money going into the top. The difference stayed in the bag and was invested in various mutual funds.

The bag represents the insurance policy. Inside of it, your extra money will grow tax-deferred until you need it for something, when you can borrow from yourself.

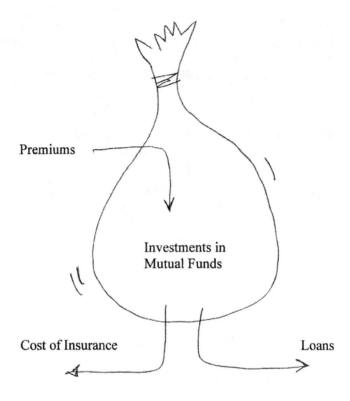

When that something comes up, like college needs, retirement needs, vacations, and so on, you can take it out of the 'bag' for yourself. It's not a formal retirement plan. Therefore, you don't report this to the government like you would money coming out of a 401(K).

"You said the money grows tax-deferred. What about when it comes out?" Pat said.

"Good question. It would be fully taxable but there's another angle to this that makes it very attractive. You can <u>borrow</u> money from your own cash value. If you do, it's not taxable."

"How much can you put in there?" Pat said.

"Lots. Let's say your premium is $100 a month. Within certain limits, you can pour hundreds of dollars into the bag. All the time, your insurance costs remain the same so the extra money goes to your investment part in the bag. And since it's your money, you don't have to pay it back if you don't want."

Pat shook her head back and forth. "This is great. How come I've never heard about this? I've never seen any magazine articles about it."

"Don't know. My guess is that it's just a little too complicated and most columnists in magazines are limited to a small space to write. They don't have the space to fully cover the subject. Once I've explained it, it's simple. But it takes a little time to educate people about what great products these can be in certain situations. This kind of insurance will create a death benefit for you, of course. But it also allows you to **create a living benefit too.** So let's review the advantages of this kind of this insurance:"

—The cash value inside a permanent life policy grows tax-deferred. When you take some of your cash value out, you are able to "borrow" from yourself

—You don't necessarily need to pay yourself, or the policy, back

—Since it's considered a loan, you don't have to pay any income taxes on money coming out of the policy

—Depending on the type of policy you own, you may be able to invest the cash value in a group of mutual funds and have your money grow at market rates, tax deferred

—You can build-up your cash value by investing more than the amount of the premium every month

—There is no Required Minimum Distribution at any time

–When you die, your beneficiary gets the Death Benefit plus any cash value from your investments. If you've borrowed from your policy, this amount will be deducted from the final number the beneficiary receives

I told them the story of two clients.

Ron and LydiaMarie have a permanent life insurance policy on LydiaMarie. They placed it on her because she is female and, therefore, will have a less expensive premium than a male. It's not term, or temporary, insurance because the investment feature is not available with term insurance. They have three grandchildren they want to help with down payments for future homes. The basic premium for LydiaMarie is $167 a month. Instead, they are putting $500 a month in the policy. That means, $333 of the payment is going not to insurance costs but to investments within the policy.

In addition, they are investing this extra cash in a group of mutual funds held within the policy. It's called a Variable Universal Life insurance policy.

Their money will grow with the market and when each grandchild gets to the point of needing a down payment, Ron and LydiaMarie can simply "borrow" it from themselves, tax-free, and give it to the grandchild. Depending on how much they give, there may be some gift tax owed, but the point is, no income taxes are owed…ever!

"But if they're borrowing it, don't they have to pay it back?"

LydiaMarie has a $250,000 death benefit. If she borrows $10,000, doesn't pay it back, and dies, her beneficiary, Ron, will get $250,000 less the $10,000 she borrowed for a total death benefit of $240,000. You don't have to "pay yourself back."

"You mean we should go out and buy life insurance before we retire?" Pat asked. She turned toward me.

"Depending on what age and how healthy you are, insurance may be very expensive at this point. We'd have to get some quotes to see if it made sense. The best way to do this is to look for any permanent policies you already own," I said. "This idea only works if you have a need for life insurance."

"What's the downside?" Charlie asked.

Permanent insurance is expensive. That's why, if you don't need insurance for other reasons, this idea isn't going to fit. But if you have a policy already, or need one and the cost isn't too high, this strategy works well.

Here's a similar idea.

The many advantages of annuities

—Annuities are like giant IOU's where you invest a sum of money in an annuity contract with an insurance company

—The money grows inside the annuity tax-deferred

—Mutual funds may be used inside the annuity

—When money is withdrawn, only the growth portion of the money is taxed

—They have a death benefit which usually guarantees that if you die, your beneficiary will receive at least the money you originally invested in the annuity. If the investments have grown more than the original investment amount, that growth is given to the beneficiary also.

—After age 59 ½, you can take out the money any way you want without penalty

—There is no Required Minimum Distribution rule

—At some point in your life, you can choose to "annuitize" the contract which means that you will receive a lifetime, monthly income based on the value of your investment and age. You can <u>never</u> outlive this stream of income

"These sound great, too," said Pam. She frowned, "What's the catch?"

Like life insurance, these contracts have higher costs. They are <u>not</u> life insurance, but there is a death benefit.

There's also another tool to use.

Roth IRA's. Remember, money invested in these grows tax-deferred and may be withdrawn after 59 ½ tax-free. In order to contribute to these, you must be working, however. On the flip side, Roth IRA's have very low costs compared to the two insurance ideas you have now.

I pushed back from the table and took a deep breath. "All of these strategies try to accomplish the same thing: to move money out of taxable accounts into non-taxable, or partially taxable ones. It's fun to try and keep as much money as you can from the government."

"I get it," Pat said. "Instead of loading up on 401(K) contributions or deferred compensation plans, we should think of funding these alternatives."

"Right. Maybe you could split it half-and-half, or three ways between taxable retirement accounts and two non-taxable alternatives. The younger you are, the better it works because by the time you have already retired, it may be too late to make these moves."

Charlie cleared his throat. "Wait a minute. We're so close to retirement, does this make any sense for us?"

"It could…maybe thousands of dollars in saved taxes for you," I said. "The strategy I recommend is to start shifting money over the next ten years…well ahead of your 70th birthday. Remember the RMD withdrawals. In addition, to keep your taxes lower as you shift this money around, it's a good idea to get a lot of it moved before you began receiving Social Security benefits. Think back to the avalanche of taxes you'll face.

You can see, that these strategies try to 'time' when you will start receiving income and whether that income is subject to income tax or not. There are very few ways to avoid paying income tax on your income, so it's vitally important to take advantage of these tools. The sooner you learn how they work and use them, the better. Once the time has run, meaning you get near age 70, it's too late for these tools to have much benefit. You will end up needlessly paying more taxes.

What my notes said

1. I started to teach them some strategies to beat the problems they would face in retirement. If they prepare, using these, they could quit working

2. I assured Charlie and Pat that this knowledge would free them from worry. They should learn how to help themselves with their money

3. I suggested, to delay using their retirement money and saved assets as long as they could. If that meant working at a part time job for a few years...okay.

4. I urged them to learn how to get the money that they already had, working harder for them

5. They could take advantage of the great benefits of Roth IRAs

6. They could look into the advantages of permanent life insurance, particularly Variable Universal Life insurance because it provided, along with life insurance, an investment opportunity. Money could grow tax-deferred inside the policy and be taken out by loans in a tax-free manner.

7. Annuities were also a good strategy to follow since money inside annuities also grew tax-deferred and money taken out was only partially taxable. Moreover, with both life insurance and annuities, they wouldn't be forced to take money out because of any Required Minimum Distribution rules from the IRS. They could have complete freedom of choice.

8. Finally, Pat and Charlie could always use a combination of strategies to fit their needs exactly and I urged them to act immediately!

Lesson Three:
Learn to stretch and grow—both you and your money—while reducing risk

Lesson Three:
Learn to stretch and grow—both you and your money—while reducing losses

Chapter Five

How can I sleep at night without worrying about my money?

A week later, at my office, I stood from the table to retrieve a small watering can. I moved close to the window and drenched each plant that stood there. I wanted to tell Charlie and Pat a story I'd read about in <u>Play to Win</u>, by Larry Wilson and Hersch Wilson, Bard Press, Austin, Texas, 1998.

> There were some cattle ranchers in Texas some years back. You can imagine that those ranches were huge. The cost of fencing everything was very expensive, particularly where the fences crossed roads. Just think of how much it would cost to build gates at every road. How would they open when people drove through and who would close them?
>
> So, they developed a neat idea. They dug a deep, square hole in the road at the point the gate crossed it. Over the hole, they laid iron bars, with spaces between them. Very solid. Now, cars could drive across the iron bars without having to stop to open a gate. And the cattle were afraid to step across these iron bars for fear their feet would fall through and they'd get stuck. Cattle aren't too bright, anyway.

Trouble was, those iron bars were rough to ride over for the trucks and cars. Especially if you were going fast..

Some smart rancher, knowing how placid and slow cattle were, decided, after awhile, to <u>paint</u> the bars on the road itself. And you know what? The cattle came up to the gate, looked at the "bars" and turned around!

Here's where risk comes in. After awhile, one enterprising cow decided to test the painted bars. I can't imagine what goes through a cow's brain, but I'm sure he didn't consciously think: "I'm going to risk falling in." Anyway, one day, the cow stepped onto the painted bars and kept going. Thanks to his taking a risk, the entire herd followed to the far greener, lush pastures that had not been opened to them before. They must've been happy to be "dining at the better restaurant".

Pat said, "So, you're telling us to take risks. But I've always heard that when you retire, you should take fewer risks."

I put down the watering can. "For most people, unfortunately, that's true. There's a simple formula I'd like you to get into your heads." I sat down and reached across the desk, picked-up the pen again, and wrote:

Stretching = Growth

"Notice I didn't use the word 'risk'? When I mention this to people, they automatically assume I'm referring to big financial risks or physical risks."

"Like bungee-jumping?" Charlie said.

"Right. Or the risk of starting your own business. All those are risks, of course, and hard. For some people, these risky things are a symbolic way of trying something new. There's lots of these activities: riding Harley's, parachuting, climbing mountains, going into politics, you know. I'm not talking about these kinds of things so much. The most difficult stretches are the internal ones, not the external ones."

The biggest stretch for most people is change. These aren't about the external things: change jobs, change homes, spouses, empty nests, or cars. The toughest changes are those we make within ourselves. Many writers and smarter people than I have described this as changing our "internal maps".

"Oh, I know what you're referring to," Pat said. "As we grow, each of us develops ways of thinking and relating to the world around us. These patterns are called 'maps' because they give us a sense of direction, of how to relate to people and things we meet every day. We have maps for everything: where we work, social, church activities, leisure times, family, partners…

"But are maps a bad thing?" Charlie asked.

"Nope. Because they help us to navigate our lives, based on our past learning and experiences," Pat said. "And we can predict, to some degree, how we should act in these situations as they come to us in the future."

Maps are essential. Problems come when people don't change their maps to fit new circumstances. In fact, psychologists say that most people's maps are established by middle age and <u>never</u> change again. That means the way they relate to the world around them is very out-of-date. Their views are narrow peepholes. People feel certain that their maps are complete and accurate. They're no longer interested in obtaining new, updated data for the creation of new maps.

"Why don't they update?" Charlie asked.

"Oh…I suppose it's a combination of habit, laziness, comfort. It's a lot of work to update your maps. Uncomfortable too, because if you do it honestly, the updating will challenge most of what you've relied upon, more or less successfully, for years."

"One of the engineers in my office says she's going to retire and that she's worked hard for forty years. Now, she just wants to relax and play golf. What's wrong with that?"

"Nothing," I said. "But what she might be really saying is: my working view of the world has been challenged for forty years—I've had to adapt, somehow, for a long time. And I don't want any more changes in my life."

"And the irony is that <u>everything</u> around us is changing—how can our old maps <u>ever</u> be accurate?" Pat said.

Our human trait of avoiding changes and challenges is very common—the vast majority of people, in fact. Then, there are the rare, few people who have the courage to face new challenges and to change their maps and to take the risks of where that transformation will lead them. It'll lead them, of course, to the freedom simply, 'to be', maybe for the first time in their lives.

"That's so wonderful and…liberating," Pat said. "but when it comes to money, we don't have an entire lifetime to work anymore. Nor, would we want to! Shouldn't we be more careful, take fewer risks? What if we screw-up something?" She looked my way again.

I offered them more mineral water along with a bowl of hard mint candy."You hit the nail on the head, Pat. We've been talking about personal growth and change. When it comes to your money, you have to take some risk to get it to grow."

Charlie interrupted, "Because of inflation? Like the postage stamps?"

"Right. I think the key word is balance. As you get older, the balance should change to less risk while still trying to maintain growth. It's as much an emotional choice as it is a financial one. And it's different for everyone."

Wheel of Fortune

I pointed out that most people plan their retirement money issues like they're replaying Wheel of Fortune: they bet everything on one or two things, hoping they'll make the right choice and win big. I gave them the example of a retired couple that came to me for advice.

Ruth was a retired school nurse and Dalton had been the city engineer for a suburban town. They were in their late 60's, had sizable IRA's, and Social Security benefits for their resources. Their house was paid-off. They had watched a TV show about the economy that worried them. In response, they sold every fund in their IRAs and traded it all for Certificates of Deposit, still in their IRAs. The CD's paid a guaranteed 2.6% interest. They wanted to know my opinion.

Why they had purchased all the CD's? Because they didn't think it was prudent for people their age to have any risk. They said the CDs were guaranteed, that there wasn't any risk. They were insured by FDIC at the bank where they had their IRAs. They admitted they wouldn't "get rich" earning 2.6% a year but at least, it was safe without risk.

Unfortunately, this couple's decision caused them to give up almost any chance for growth. They were in good health and could live for another twenty years or more. They needed growth to keep up with inflation… the postage stamps. But even after they gave up their opportunities for growth, they didn't really trade for low risk.

Inflation doesn't go away. It's averaged 3.1%. That means, if they earn 2.6% and inflation continues to average 3.1%, this couple will be driving in reverse! They won't "floor it" but it'll be backwards. They simply moved from one type of risk—in the market—to another type of risk, because they weren't getting enough growth to stay ahead of inflation. Some risk is necessary, particularly for the unseen costs of things in the next thirty years.

A three-layer cake

"I'm going to tell you about three-layer cakes. And that reminds me we need a break. There's the deli downstairs." I glanced at my watch. "I think we can still catch something."

We took the elevator down to the lobby of the building. Next to the lobby, the deli rested in the spring sun falling from the huge skylights above. Green fronds from potted plants stretched their arms around the eating area. We went to the counter. Pam ordered a fruit plate. Charlie and I each chose a thin…very thin slice of cheesecake drenched in raspberry sauce. At the end of the counter, we ordered coffee and lattes.

We sat in comfortable chairs below the skylights.

I started with the metaphor, "three-layer cake". Simply, it means that you should divide your savings and investments into three groups: short-term, inter-mediate-term, and long-term assets. The amount in each group will vary accord-ing to your individual circumstances.

"Give us an example," Pat asked. She frowned when she looked at the cheese-cake in front of me and the puddle of raspberry sauce. I smiled back at her.

The older you are, the more you may want to put into the short-term layer in case you have emergencies or the value of your other investments dip in a down market. Each layer has a different purpose. Remember, you're trying to reduce risk and that comes from three possible things:

1. An emergency that could wipe-out your retirement savings
2. Once you start taking an income from your investments, if the market drops, you could be forced to dip-into your principal
3.. As we talked about before, you still need your investments to keep growing but you don't want to bet the farm on the newest "hot" fund.

With each layer, you could we invest more aggressively. So that, in the long-term group, we could try to get good growth. Your short-term funds could go into money market funds, savings, CD's, short-term bonds, and other safe places. You won't get much growth but your money will be safe and easily accessible whenever you need it."

"Okay," Charlie said, "the big question: how much?"

"For you folks, for instance, once you retire, if either of you is working part-time, you don't need a lot in there. For older folks, they might need a year or two saved in short term reserves."

"That much? It sounds like a lot to me."

We're trying to avoid a second risk—down markets that drain our resources. I spread-out my napkin and pulled out a felt-tip pen. I drew around smudges of raspberry. Here's an example.

Retired couple: Fred and Wilma

Investments: $600,000 in an IRA

Income needs: $30,000/year (5% withdrawal)

(Most economists say you can safely take a 5% income from an investment without depleting the asset or "dipping into your principal", although I said it's a little more complicated than that. We'll talk about it later.)

So long as there's a bull market and it's rising, Fred and Wilma won't have any problems maintaining their level of income and assets. But look what happens if a bear market continues for a few years.

Year 1 $600,000 - $30,000 = $570,000 and market drops 10% so Fred and Wilma are left with: $513,000

Year 2 $513,000 - $30,000 = $483,000 and market drops 10% so Fred and Wilma are left with: $434,700

Year 3 $434,700 - $30,000 = $404,700 and this year, the market only drops 5%, leaving Fred and Wilma with: $384,465 (at the beginning of the 4th year)

Since the market has been dropping, they were forced to take their income out of the principal. Just to get themselves back to where they started at $600,000, they would need to grow their money by more than 50%! Even when the market turns around and rises, they will still take $30,000 a year from their IRA, so it looks like it would be impossible for them to recover.

Had they layered a year or two of income needs into short-term accounts, they could've drawn from those until the market improved, preserving their value in the IRA. The other strategy I proposed was to put the intermediate money in funds that are balanced between growth and preservation of capital. The long-term money should be invested into growth funds. When Fred and Wilma experienced bull markets and their intermediate or long-term funds were up, they could draw-off some of those funds and add them to the short-term reserves, which would prepare them for the times when the market went down, as it inevitably does.

Charlie pushed his small, empty plate to the side as he finished the example. He swirled his latte in the cup and sipped it.

Another consideration here is something called "liquidity priority." It's just a way of looking at which investments you cash-in first to minimize the tax bite and to allow the tax-deferred accounts to keep growing as long as possible. This reduces the risk of taxes chewing-up your resources.

"That makes sense," Pat said. "So, you would take money out of your IRAs last. Because they are tax-deferred, you'd want to let that run as long as you could?"

"Sure. Here's a typical example of the retired clients I have:"

Fred and Wilma have the following:

1. Taxable mutual funds (non-retirement accounts)
2. Stocks and bonds that have increased in value
3. An IRA
4. A Roth IRA

Suggested strategy:

1. Cash in the taxable mutual funds
2. Liquidate the stocks and take long-term capital gain tax rates (which are lower than income tax rates)
3. Take money from the IRA
4. Cash-in the Roth IRA

"Even if a couple did this more than a twenty to thirty year period, they would save tremendously on taxes and reduce the risk of losing that money to taxes." I said.

"I'll <u>never</u> go to a nursing home!"

"Come on, let's hike back to the office," I said.

"Oh…let's not. It's so nice here." Pat protested. We sat in the slanting sun from the skylights. Between food, coffee, and the sun, it was warm in the deli.

Looking at Long Term Care insurance.

Charlie squirmed and made a sour face. "I don't know…. Is it really worth it? Most of the columns I've read in the magazines really question the value of it."

"Let me tell you a story," I said. "then, you tell me if it's worth it."

They both nodded and listened.

I had an aunt and uncle, named Butch and Ellie. They both had excellent health for years. Then, when Ellie was in her early seventies, she started acting weird. She would become violently angry with Butch, accusing him of having affairs with other women. During conversations about going to the mall, she would interject stories about riding the streetcars. She forgot many things, was unable to care for herself. At the time, everyone called it dementia. Today, we'd recognize it as Alzheimer's.

My uncle was a few years older than Ellie and in good health himself. He had been and always was, devoted to my aunt and started to try to care for her. Some days he just couldn't hack it. Partly because of his age and partly because it was so emotionally tough. She yelled at him without warning and accused him of the craziest things.

My father and his siblings had to intervene to help Butch. The family started around-the-clock care of Ellie. All of them had to interrupt their own lives and families to care for Ellie. Butch's health declined. After two years, Ellie died. Butch, who had been a very healthy man, died less than two years after she did. Both suffered in the process. It took on everyone, not just Butch.

"Couldn't they use Medicare?" Pat asked.

"Medicare doesn't cover things like this and no, they didn't have other insurance."

Another common situation with my clients is like my friend Peter. He is 84 and had been in good health. Thanks to the snowy, icy winters here in Minnesota, he fell last winter and broke his hip. He was bedridden for months while he recovered and went through rehab to learn to walk again. He's okay now, but the process drained 80% of he and his wife's assets. At 76, she had to go back to work at Wal Mart.

"What do these stories have to do with nursing homes?" asked Charlie.

"No client has ever told me they'd like to go into a nursing home. Never! But these examples are more common than you think. You've probably got stories like this in your families."

Long-term care insurance will pay for nursing home stays, of course. But much more common is the need for in-home care or assisted care facilities. It's estimated that by the year 2020, 12 million older Americans will need long-term care of some sort. Most will be cared for, like my aunt, at home. Family members and friends will be the sole care givers for 70% of elderly people. A study by the U.S. Department of Health and Human Services indicates that people over age 65 face at least a 40% lifetime risk of entering a nursing home. The figure for people needing assisted care or home care is much higher No one wants to go to a nursing home. Good, long-term care insurance policies help you to stay out of a nursing home.

"So it's obvious that many of us will probably need some kind of home care," Pat said.

"Sure," I said. "and it's not cheap unless the family is willing and able to do it all."

Pat turned to me. "This is primarily a woman's issue. I know many, many women who have had better health than their husbands and have had to spend time and energy caring for them in the end. But if I'm 80 when this problem arises, I may not have the energy or ability to do it." She turned to Charlie. "I can only imagine how expensive this kind of care is…"

Specialized, trained care-givers, nurses, rehab experts are very costly. The national average for a year's stay in a nursing home runs more than $60,000 depending on what area of the country you're in. Assisted care and home care are probably cheaper, but still can cost a fortune. We looked at the example of Fred and Wilma with their $600,000 IRA. What if they took out $30,000 a year for living expenses and then needed an additional $40,000 a year to help Fred remain at home during some illness?

"So we need long-term care insurance?" Charlie asked.

Generally speaking, you can reduce the risk of losing your money by investing in a policy for each of you. What people don't get is that these policies cover nursing home stays, of course, but they 'll also pay for assisted care facilities and home health care, too. They can help you stay out of a nursing home.

"People hope Medicare or the government is somehow going to pay for these problems. They don't."

People who should seriously look at this type of insurance are:

1.   Are in their early 50's to 84

2.   Have significant assets that they want to protect

3.   Can afford to pay the premiums now and in the future

4.   Are in good health and are insurable."

"How does it work, then?" Pat said.

To understand these, remember it's an insurance policy. You pay premiums until a certain event occurs, then the company will pay you a daily dollar amount that you previously agreed to in the policy. These "events" are when a person can't perform two or more of the "activities of daily living" or is impaired because of Alzheimer's disease. Activities like, bathing, dressing, getting from a bed to a chair (for instance), going to the toilet, eating, and continence.

If a person can't do two or more of these activities, the insurance company will pay a daily, dollar amount. Let's say you contracted for $200 a day. Once the money starts flowing, with many of these policies, you could take that $200 and purchase the services you needed at home, including rehab help and equipment, meal preparation, respite care, nursing, cleaning help and so on. You can also get inflation protection so the daily dollar amount rises each year. Each policy is different, of course.

"I just hear the coins falling out of our pockets," Pat said. "These have got to be really expensive. Those services aren't cheap!"

It's the biggest hurdle for most people. It's not cheap. But there are ways to reduce the cost. And of course, people always ask, "is it worth it?"

Compare it to your homeowner's insurance. Hopefully, your house never burns down and you never need it. You would have paid for it all the time you lived in the house and received nothing in return. Is it worth it? What if, by some wild chance, your house burns down? Is it worth it then? Of course. That's the 'deal' with insurance companies.

The other thing to consider when reviewing the price of these policies is the "cost" to your retirement funds if you are forced to dip into them. For instance, if you've planned for thirty years of retirement and a long term care emergency hits you that takes two years and 25% of your assets to recover, that loss in your retirement assets could jeopardize your income sources for the rest of your life. Something, you could never recover from. Long term care insurance pays for these care costs so that you don't have to dip into your retirement assets.

"You said there are ways to keep the cost of long-term care insurance down," Pat reminded me.

For one thing, people who don't have many assets probably don't need this anyway. For those who do have assets and want to protect from losing them to a health care expenses, can use some of their own assets to pay a portion of the health care costs, if they arise.

"Give us an example."

Look at car insurance. When you choose a $250 deductible, your insurance will cost so much. But if you raise your deductible to $1,000, meaning you'll pay the first $1,000 of damages, the cost of insurance drops. Same here. The higher the deductible the cheaper the policy.

"So if the cost of an assisted care facility is $200 a day and we're willing and able to pay $75 of that per day, we would only need a policy that paid us $125 a day?"

In addition, you could delay the time period that the benefits start flowing. Instead of getting the daily dollar amount immediately when the need arises, you could tell the insurance company to wait 30, 60, or 180 days, for instance. The longer you wait and use your own money, the less expensive the policy will be.

"Then what's the use of having it in the first place?" Charlie asked.

"In Pat's example, you would depend on it for the large, long-term expenses for health problems. It'd cost you a little every day but you wouldn't run the risk of wiping-out all your savings and retirement money."

Another way to save on the cost is to reduce the benefit period. The daily dollar amount will flow, uninterrupted for as long as you agreed with the insurance company. It can be for a period of 2,3, 5 years or for the rest of the person's life. Obviously, the longer the benefit period is, the more expensive. And when you consider that the average stay in a nursing home is about three years, you may not need a longer period.

Pat said, "But Colin, don't women live longer than men?"

"Of course. I said the average stay is about three years, but when you look at men, the time is shorter. I can't remember for sure, but I think it's about two years and for women about four years. Not sure."

"Do we pay the same premium every year?"

"Depending on your age and your health when you purchase it, yes. That's why it's a good idea to start looking at these policies when you're in your 50's or 60's. By the time you are 70, the costs blast through the roof."

Pat asked, "Are there any alternatives to long-term care insurance?"

"Some. Life insurance is generally cheaper than long-term care insurance. A couple could purchase two life insurance policies, one on each of their lives. It'd work like this:"

Fred and Wilma have $1.75 million in assets. Fred gets injured and needs some home health care for 14 months. This couple could probably pay for all of Fred's care out of their own money and still have enough left over to support themselves in retirement. Years later, when Fred dies, Wilma will inherit the life insurance death benefit and would be able to replenish the retirement funds, used for Fred's care.

Many people have smaller amounts in retirement funds but have paid off their house. They could use a reverse mortgage to get at funds to pay for these costs as an alternative to buying long-term care insurance.

"Couldn't we just spend everything and have the state pay for a nursing home? I mean, I'm not sure I'll really care at that point where I am." Charlie said.

That's called Medicaid. First of all, you really have to spend down almost <u>everything</u> you have. There would be nothing left to live on. You both would be on welfare. Besides, if you were on Medicaid and needed a nursing home, you wouldn't have much of a choice which one you went to. The government would pick one for you depending on where the openings were that they had. Can you trust yourself to them? The quality of care varies from state to state so if you were in a state with poor care, it could be very rough.

Be sure to prepare a Will for yourselves. It can be quite simple. It acts like a road map to tell your family where you want money and things to go after you die. It reduces the risk that your assets won't go to where and to whom you want them to go. Especially, if have children, it's important to pick someone to raise them, if they're minors, and someone to administer the money you leave them until they become old enough to handle it themselves. If a person has large assets and faces potential tax problems, a Will and estate planning can, in most cases, minimize these problems. A very practical reasons involves what's called personal property. Often, we want to give certain special items to certain people. If you don't indicate that in your will, that person may never get the item you wanted them to have. Families often disagree more over the small things and who will keep them, than the large issues of assets.

Equally important these days is a Living Will. It's different from a will in that it gives instructions to your family and friends on how to handle end-of-life questions about yourself, particularly medical questions. It's designed to cover situations when you are still alive but may not be able to make decisions for yourself. The classic case involves those people in "vegetative states" and the decision of when to remove life-support measures. If done ahead of time, it makes these problems so much easier for your family to handle. They can make these difficult decisions, even if they don't agree, because you instructed them to do it.

Another legal document that's vital is a Pre-nuptial Agreement. This is useful for people who are remarrying who also have children and assets from a previous marriage. Many times each one of the new partners wants his/her assets to stay with the children from the first marriage. Without a Pre-nuptial Agreement, upon the death of one of the partners, his/her assets could go to the children of the other, new partner. These used to be common for Hollywood stars on their fourth and fifth marriages but today, are common for many people.

What my notes said

1. I emphasized the importance of stretching, growing, and changing our "maps" of the way life and the world around each of us works.

2. I taught them not to use the "Wheel of Fortune" with their money. Don't bet on one thing only, and not be willing to learn and change, if necessary. It helps to reduce potential losses and prepares people for the natural ups and downs of their investments.

3. The "Three Layer Cake" means to divide their money into different investment resources for different time frames. This way, if emergencies arise, they've got the ability to go through it without great risk.

4. I stressed the importance of investing in Long Term Care insurance to reduce the risk of running through all their money because of medical/health care costs.

5. I urged them to prepare both a Will and Living Wills for themselves, to provide road maps for their family. If the situation called for it, a Prenuptial Agreement was important too.

Chapter Six

Don't put all your eggs in one basket

For our next lesson, I suggested we drive over to the St. Paul Conservatory. Spring was coming but still, with Minnesota's climate, the greenery of the Conservatory was inviting.

We met in the parking lot in early afternoon. A blue sky stretched over us and, in the distance, white balls of clouds piled-up as if there were mountains beneath them. We discovered it was warmer than expected We stopped at a coffee kiosk and decided to start our lesson outside the Conservatory at some tables, sheltered by a wing of the building. Later, we could tour inside. We planted ourselves around the metal table. Without a word, all of us leaned back to feel the sun on our faces.

"What's on the stove for us today?" asked Charlie.

Don't Put All Your Eggs in One Basket

I laughed. "All right, if you insist, the formal word: diversification." It's our lesson today because we're still learning how to reduce risk with your money."

"Makes sense…the not all your eggs part, I mean," Pat said.

"In some ways, that's how simple is; in other ways, it's very sophisticated." I paused. "But first things first."

Diversification–what's the idea behind it, the theory, and is there any proof it works?

Regardless of what the "experts" say on TV or in the media, no one knows for sure what investments will go up or which ones will go down. The economy's too big, too many players, too many other factors. The purpose of much of the programming in the media is for entertainment, not education. They really don't care if you get rich or not, so long as you keep buying their magazines or watching their channels. Some of the information is valid, but even so, it's generic. It's aimed at <u>every</u> viewer. It may not apply to a person's specific situation or even be helpful for that person.

"That's for sure," Pat said. "They're more concerned that you don't click to a new channel."

I pulled out a chart from my briefcase, pushed my cup to the side, and spread the chart before us. It consisted of a series of colored boxes that resembled a chess board.

It was covered with little, square boxes of different colors. Inside each box were labels that represented different sectors of the market: small companies, bonds, large companies. Along the left side were rankings from the top, or best performing, to the bottom, the worst performing. Across the top were the past years.

Fund Sector Performance

Ranking	1998	1999	2000
1st	Russell 1000 Growth	Russell 2000 Growth	Equity REITS
2nd		Russell 1000 Growth	
7th	Russell 2000 Growth		
9th (out of 9)	Equity REITS	Equity REITS	Russell 2000 Growth

"Colorful," Charlie said.

"Each box stands for an index, that are the average returns for that type of investment," I said. "See…here's the Russell 2000: small companies. Here's the MSCI EAFE index: which are international stocks, see? Look at this, at 1998."

They did. The best performer was the Russell 1000 Growth index—made up of large, blue-chip companies.

"Now look at 2000."

They did. The Russell 1000 fell to almost the worst performance for the year.

"Look at the top winner: Equity REITs. Those are investments in real estate."

They followed my finger back and down to 1999. Equity REITs came in dead last!

I sat back. "Here's what happens to the majority of people. It's the problem with following the advice from the media, too. Let me tell you a story."

Years ago I found myself talking to the owner of a small but successful autorepair shop. Many of them make lots of money and have large retirement plans.

The owner, Tom, told me flat-out he couldn't see any reason why he'd possibly need my advice, much less pay for it. Curious, I asked him why. "Well, it's easy," he told me. "I just look at the latest issue of 'Money' magazine and find the top mutual funds. I buy 'em. If they don't grow by at least 20%, I dump 'em the next year and buy the new winners."

Let's suppose he loaded-up his 401(K) at the end of 1998 with large, blue-chip stocks—the Russell 1000. In '98 they had exploded with growth of 38.7%! Tom's happy and hangs in there and gets 33.1% growth through '99. But by the end of 2000, he's lost 22.4% and so he dumps them.

"He'll start all over again," I said, "always chasing last year's performance."

Charlie nodded. "Worse than that, Colin. Look what he's paying. At the end of '98 everyone else wanted the Russell 1000 funds, like Tom. Prices for those funds skyrocketed. Like Tom, everyone dumped them at the end of 2000, when prices had crashed."

"So, he's buying 'high' and selling 'low'?"

"Yes—the exact opposite of what you should do to get ahead," I said.

Pat shook her head. "But why? It's so obvious not to do that!"

We invest largely on emotional impulses. We like to go with the winners and get scared with losers. Many, many people look at their 401(K)'s in early January and see a fund that's gone down. They're afraid they're 'losing' money so they sell and look for last year's winner. Like Tom, they move all their money to the new fund.

In addition, the media feeds into this normal human tendency by constantly promoting the "top performers" as if this was a horse race. They do it in order to sell next month's magazine. Each month, they can list the top funds. The problem occurs when investors follow these funds by switching from one to the other again and again.

To protect against this normal, human reaction, Asset Allocation models were developed. There's an interesting story behind its development. In 1990, three economists won the Nobel Prize—Miller, Moscowitz, and Sharpe—for their years' of academic research. They weren't paid by the mutual fund industry. They were trying to answer an old question. If a person has a portfolio of funds, in a 401(K), for instance, what are the factors that lead to success? Of course, there have been thousands of books written on how to "beat the market", but these researchers tried to use rigorous, unbiased data to answer the question. They studied it for years. Thanks to the increased power of computers, they were able to run hundreds of thousands of comparisons from historical data on the performance of different funds and types of stocks.

They were looking for patterns. To find which winners most often matched with which losers. And which ones behaved the <u>opposite</u> of each other. It was really the opposite behavior they were most interested in finding. The technical words are: negative correlation.

I pointed to the chart again. "Look: in '98 the top winner was the Russell 1000, worst loser—Equity REITs. But…in year 2000 the top winner is Equity REITs and…" my finger moved down. "On the bottom is Russell 1000!"

The little chart flashed as if it had neon lights. The main point is: if a person didn't want to put all their eggs in one basket, how about two baskets? And how about two that behaved exactly opposite of each other? Whichever one wins, the investor will be covered.

"You said they ran thousands of comparisons…did they find more than two that worked opposite?"

Thanks to the computers and their brains, they found several, optimal combinations. Then, they developed a software program that's available to investors today. It's a very simple idea that's backed by years of sophisticated research—all to confirm what we know anyway: don't put all your eggs in one basket.

Ironically, the financial media still keeps trying to sell the idea that <u>their</u> particular funds are better than others. They do this primarily by emphasizing last year's returns, which they claim proves they have the "right" investment that the consumer must buy. They advertise that if you specialize and only buy their funds, you'll become rich and successful. That's not what the academic research shows. So, the media can be very misleading, at times.

What strategies make your investments successful?

Thirty years of economic research using the true, historical data, showed that financial success in a portfolio was due to the following things.

1 ½% due to which funds or stocks/bonds you buy

1 ½% due to when you buy or sell

97% due to Asset Allocation.

Not only did the economists show Asset Allocation to be so important for growth but it also reduces risk. An investor, following a personalized Asset Allocation model, will have his/her investments spread over a range of different choices. These choices will be determined by the logical, analytical research already done, rather than "tips" for certain funds that people often receive over coffee or on the financial news shows.

Investors answer a series of questions that are designed to measure their desire for growth matched to their tolerance for risk. These answers are entered into the computer and a personalized model is created for the investor to follow. It shows the optimum balance of funds for that investor. And the software creates a picture, usually a pie chart, that gives the percentages the investor should place in each category. Here's one prepared by Thompson Financial Blueprint, 2002.

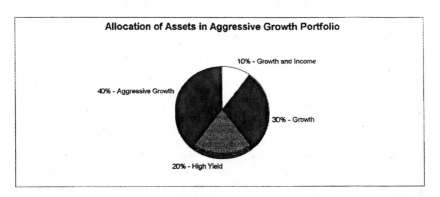

The chart can be changed, depending on how the investor answers the questions. For instance, one of the questions usually is: When do you plan to start withdrawing money from your accounts?" If a person had retired, the answer will change to: immediately. The chart will also change accordingly, to reflect this new aspect. Other questions ask about the investor's age, their sense of how much risk they're willing to take on, or how long will their money have to last once they start drawing from it.

So, for each stage of a person's life, the model will change to reflect the changes in their lives. It makes investing not only easier, but it removes the normal, human emotional responses from the decision of where to put the money.

It answers that question, too. Where should I put my investments?

Once you follow the model and balance your investments, you only need to re-balance about once a year. In the meantime, you don't need to worry. When a crises hits, you can relax, knowing that you have "your eggs" spread over many baskets to reduce your risk. Perhaps, this is the greatest aspect of Asset Allocation: it eliminates a lot of the worry and concern people have about their investments, particularly when they hear bad financial news in the media.

What does "rebalancing" mean?

Here's a simple example. I pulled the green pen from my pocket. I started to draw a simple Asset Allocation model.

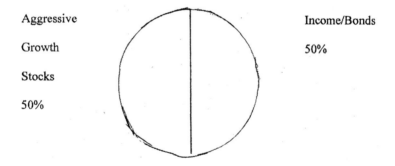

Aggressive

Growth

Stocks

50%

Income/Bonds

50%

"Let's keep it very simple, okay? This is your Asset Allocation model. You have half your money in aggressive growth stock funds, and half in income and bond funds. During the year, these funds will go up or down. At the end of the first year, here's what you've got."

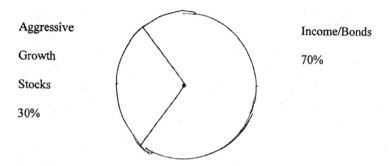

Aggressive

Growth

Stocks

30%

Income/Bonds

70%

What should you do with your investments? It becomes very simple: you should sell 20% of your income/bond funds and buy 20% more aggressive growth stock funds to get your balance back to 50% in each category. Obviously, in a real Asset Allocation model, the percentages will be more complicated and may involve more balancing, but the principle is the same. You want to get back to the original balance for each category.

"But Colin, if bonds have been growing, why should we sell 'em? Why would we sell the 'winners' in order to buy the 'losers'?" Charlie asked.

Good question. Think back to the auto repair shop owner, Tom. He bought low and sold high. Backwards. Here's another chart to explain the wisdom of rebalancing.

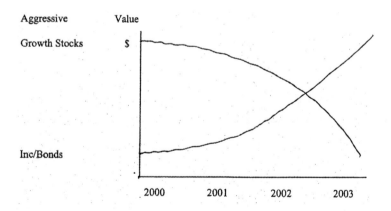

Aggressive

Growth Stocks

Value

$

Inc/Bonds

2000   2001   2002   2003

"I'm sure you remember the recession in 2000 that lasted for a few years," I said. "Stocks that had soared in the late 90's dropped like rocks during this time."

If investors weren't following Asset Allocation and rebalancing every year, they would have lost anywhere from 40–70% of the value of their aggressive growth stock fund's value. Rebalancing <u>forces</u> us to make some simple but profound decisions about our investments. On the chart above, if you look at the year 2002, you find that stocks have dropped in value. But bond values are up. That puts you in the position of the earlier circles we looked at. Now, your balance is: income/bond funds at 70% and aggressive growth stock funds at 30%. We sell 20% of the bonds and buy 20% more stocks. In this way, we're selling at a profit, selling high that is, and buying at a <u>sale price</u>, buying low.

Pat's face lit-up. "Oh! I can't believe this is so simple when you show us. Instead of following our emotional impulses, we're forced to do the smart things with our money—'buy low, sell high.'"

"Thanks to the economists that did years of research. I won't bore you with their 'efficient frontier' analysis, but bottom line is: if you follow Asset Allocation modeling, you can improve your growth and reduce your risk," I said.

Charlie stood up. "I don't know, Colin…everything I've ever heard or read…nobody ever talked about this idea before…I don't know if I swallow it all. Oh, I've seen lots of columnists say to diversify. But this sounds too good." He walked around the table in frustration.

A slight breeze brought warm air from inside the Conservatory swirling around us.

"Think of this, Charlie." I said, "if your favorite financial magazine told you in the January issue that all you had to do was follow your model and come back in January next year to rebalance, would you buy the issues for February, March, April, and so on?"

"No."

"That's the point," Pat said. "What would they have left to sell in order to get you to buy the next month's issue?"

The idea of diversification applies in our lives all the time. If you've worked at one type of job for most of your life, diversify. Change to a new line of work. If you've always listened to rock music, try something new. Don't get rid of old friends, but try to make new ones, ones that are different from your old ones. Listen to different political viewpoints rather than the ones you've heard. Purposely try to cultivate people of differing viewpoints than your own. Take on things that you don't always feel comfortable doing.

"It makes sense. I'd be open to something like that but I just don't seem to have the time. Or, I don't think about it when we're looking for something to do on a Saturday night," Pat said.

"You have to make a conscious decision. But I can tell you that in the hundreds of people I've counseled about retirement, it's so important to grow, to expand yourselves. People who don't grow become very narrow and their lives are small and usually boring and sad. So, diversify! If nothing else, it'll keep your mind active and challenged and that leads to a healthier life. You'll find that life can become richer and more exciting than perhaps ever before. Trust me."

We all decided to take a break and walk inside the Conservatory. Built almost a century ago, it was a white frame building with a circular rotunda in the middle, capped by a clear dome. Compared to the mega-theme parks dotting the country, the Conservatory remained quaint and small. Inside, the humidity steamed-up my glasses for a few minutes. I breathed in deeply of the warm, moist air. Stately palms soared to the top of the dome while others squatted near the ground. From the north wing, we heard the songs and callings of birds.

We strolled along the path that curved beneath the dripping palm fronds and found ourselves in the middle of the rotunda. In the center splashed a small fountain with the statue of a young nude girl, dancing on a wave. We sat on one of the benches at the edge. All of us, including the nude girl, were sheltered from sight by dense, green foliage growing all around us. Other than the splash of the water, it was peaceful.

We sat silently, absorbing the surroundings. I heard many things: birds calling from different parts of the building, the whirr of fans high above, soft murmurs of other voices coming from behind the ferns, falling water. I was almost able to "hear" the plants growing around me.

What my notes said

1. I emphasized not to put "all your eggs in one basket," something that sounded simple. As a result, people tended to dismiss the advice as too elementary. But it is vitally important to everyone.

2. I proved to them, with historic charts, that no one can really predict what the winners in the market will be and which ones will be the losers every year. In fact, they saw that many of last year's winners were the next year's poorest performers. They learned how to take advantage of these ups and downs.

3.   I taught them what Asset Allocation meant and how is was developed by several economists. It fit my advice for not putting all their eggs in one basket by providing a model, tailored to each person's sense of risk and growth. By following the model in their investment decisions, they could take advantage of the growth, while reducing risk.

4.   Strategies for success with investments depended more than 90% on the faithful use of an Asset Allocation model for their choices. I reminded them it was also necessary to rebalance their investment choices once a year

Chapter Seven

"We hope the market goes <u>up</u> the rest of our lives!"

Charlie's voice echoed around my office. "Why does the market have to go down? What I'm worried about is, if we quit working and the market goes down for a long time, what do we do?"

"Studies have shown that in the last 75 years or so, stocks have grown at an average of 10.4% a year. That means, your money would've doubled every seven years," I said.

"But the market still doesn't go up like a bank account where the interest you earn steadily climbs," Pat said.

"Of course not. It's more like a staircase: a series of steps. Up, level-off, drop a little, up, up. You don't get the sense of any upward progress until you look at charts for twenty, thirty years and you see the climb upward."

"I know it doesn't work this way," Charlie said, "but wouldn't we be better-off if the market did climb steadily, with no dips downward after we retired?"

We hope the market goes <u>up</u> the rest of our lives

"Can I throw-out another technical word?" I asked. "**Volatility**, the ups and-downs of the market."

It's been a fact of markets since people first started trading. Why it happens is a tough question. Doctoral theses by the truckloads have been written to try and explain it. More important, to try and predict the turns of the market. There are even 'schools' of theorists who 'chart' the ups and downs to try and predict which way the market will move.

There are probably dozens of reasons that cause the market to move one way oranother. Regardless of what the "experts" say, no one can predict market moves consistently. Some people can get a few ups and downs correctly, but to do this for a long time, is very difficult. All that has been proved for certain is that the market will gyrate and go up and down. Is there anyway we can take advantage of the certainty that the market will bounce up and down?

While people are working and have many years left before they retire, this volatility is bothersome and a big drop in the market can cause some sleepless nights. But at least, these working people have time to recover before they retire. They have time to wait until the market comes back up again. For people who have quit working and have begun to take money out of their investments, like an IRA, market drops in the value of their money, are distressing. Why can't the market always go up?

The only thing we can be sure of is that the market <u>will</u> go up and down. It will have volatility. Is there a way to take advantage of the ups and downs, even if we don't know when they're coming?

"What I don't understand," said Pat, "is how can we ever make money when the markets go down? Don't we lose money then? Every quarter when my friends at work get their statements of their 401(k)'s they can see quite clearly if they've gone down. And believe me, it doesn't feel good!"

"Especially as you get closer to retirement. If you're thirty and it drops, okay. You figure you've got time to ride it up again. But the day before you retire, if your IRA drops, that's scary. I think it's why a lot of people are afraid to retire."

"First, we should talk about the time <u>before</u> you retire. I've got some news that'll make you feel like a genius." I said. "When you're working and contributing to your retirement accounts, volatility is one of your best friends. It will always make you a winner."

"Always?"

"If you're contributing every month——always."

"Have we been doing that?" Pat asked, but I could tell that she wasn't too sure. She asked anyway as she usually does.

It's called, '**dollar cost averaging**'.

It's simple but like so many things about your money, once you learn them and practice them, they become very powerful. It just means that every month, you contribute the same to your savings or retirement accounts. But remember, every month the market is going up or down. If it went up <u>all</u> the time, you'd do well. But the fact it goes down every once in awhile, makes you look brilliant.

"I don't get it," Charlie said.

"Let me draw it." I slid closer to them on the bench and flattened a piece of paper on the table. The green, felt-tip came out again and I scratched away.

Share Price

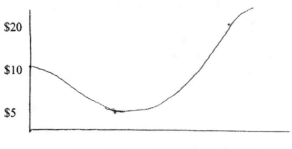

I sat back. "Let's suppose you invest $100 every month, starting in January. Notice that in January your $100 bought you 10 shares @ $10/share. But here: by March, the price dropped to $5/share. Now how many shares do you buy with $100?"

"Twenty," Pat said.

"And in June, when the price rises to $20/share, how many shares do you buy?"

"Five."

"Oh?" Pat raised her eyebrows at me. She turned back to me. "I think I get it. When the price is low, or 'on sale' as you say, we buy a greater number of shares. When the price gets expensive, we don't buy as many."

Again, the process is quite simple but the effects are quite profound. Even if, at the end of the year, the 'average' price of the fund turns out to be $10, you've really paid less because you bought a greater number of shares at the lower prices that grew to have higher value. So, while you're working and contributing, you <u>absolutely want</u> volatility. You can make money with volatility.

"So when I'm at work and everyone is complaining about their bombed-out 401(K)'s because the market's dropped, I should feel good?" Pat said.

"If you're still contributing every month."

When you're saving and the market goes down, you usually have time to recover. But when you quit working, it's an entirely different problem. For instance, the average time it takes the market to reach the previous high is 18–36 months. Not long—-if you're working. In addition, you're still buying at lower prices. If you've stopped working and are drawing money out of your IRA for instance, instead of contributing to it every month, when the market drops for an extended time, you have a problem. If the retired couple has to sell some funds to live on when the market is down, they'd be "selling low". The next year, if the market is still down, they are forced again, to sell something to live on. And since it could go on for three years or so, it just gets worse.

Until they run out of money. But remember, you still need <u>growth</u> in assets after you retire because many people will live into their 90's. Lots of people don't understand how tough a market drop is to recover from.

What it takes to recover from drops in the market

20% decline requires a…25% gain to get back to starting level

33% decline requires a…50% gain to get back to starting level

50% decline requires a…100% gains to get back to starting level

67% decline requires a…200% gain to get back to starting level

People are concerned mostly about rises in the market. They eagerly scan each quarterly report to see how much their holdings have risen. They don't realize that drops in the market, are probably more critical for their long-term success than the growth.

The emphasis is always on growth, usually ignoring the devastating effects of losses on a person's portfolio. The ability to minimize losses is, in the long run, more critical that growth.

If a person had $100 in their account and it dropped by 50%, they'd have $50 remaining. However, an increase in their holdings of 50%, the following year, will <u>not</u> get them back to their starting point. Why? Because now, they are starting with only $50. A 50% growth rate gets them to $75 at the end of the year. They would need a whopping 100% growth rate, just to get them back to where they started. And, of course, in the years it takes to get back up to the original $100, they will lose out on the potential growth their $100 could have achieved. If they started with $100 and only lost 20% of their holdings, they'd be left with $80. Now, to get back to their starting point, they only need to grow their investments by 25%—much easier than trying to grow 100%.

Minimizing losses is actually more important that maximizing growth.

Pat said, "Amazing…I never thought about it like that. So if my 401(K) drops 33%, I need more than a 33% increase to even get back where I was originally. What can we do?"

Monte Carlo Analysis

"What's a Monte Carlo analysis?" Charlie said. "Sounds exotic but risky. Makes me think of gambling."

It's got nothing to do with gambling. In fact, it was used years ago during the Manhattan Project—you know when they created the atom bomb—when they had access to computers the size of several rooms. I guess the reason they used the words "Monte Carlo" is that the program established **probabilities** that certain events would occur.

The program used to require a warehouse-sized computer. Luckily, the PC's are powerful enough now to handle these programs. Still, they're really sophisticated and actually perform thousands of calculations to answer our questions.

What about 90+% of the software used today? Although Monte Carlo analysis is available, lots of people don't know about it or understand how much better and more accurate it is. The old planning, or more common financial planning, relied on assumptions of **averages** in the variables. That is, for growth rates, inflation rates, and withdrawal rates. For instance, we'd assume that inflation would "average" 3.5% for the next thirty years. Then, we'd plug in that average to the software program. But "averages" are only that: averages. They don't cover the true fluctuations of these numbers. In real life, inflation is not 3.5% every month and every year. It fluctuates. And depending on when you want to start drawing money out of your retirement accounts, inflation may be low or high. How can we take these changes into account?

Here's an interesting example about the stock market that is found in Terry Savage's book, The Savage Number, 2005.

> From: The early 80's   to the   early 90's:
>   The Dow Jones started at about 800 and remained at 800
> From: The early 90's   to   1999:
>   The Dow Jones climbed to over 10,000

If you were to take the "average" return on stocks for the period from the early 90's to 1999, you'd get almost a 12% growth rate on the average. But obviously, the period during the 80's experienced almost no growth.

"I get it," Pat said, "in real life, there's no such thing as 'average'. For instance, if someone had retired in 1982 expecting the average growth rate of her portfolio to grow at 12%…" She shook her head. "It would've been brutal."

Not only brutal, she would've had a good chance of running out of money! A Monte Carlo program can take all these variables like growth rates, inflation rates, and income goals and project a variety of outcomes depending on how the variables are combined. They can be combined in different ways. The program relies on historical records of how inflation, for instance, behaved at many different times in the past. Or, it can look to the historical behavior of different classes of stocks and bonds—like large cap, international, long-term bonds—instead of the averages of these classes. By varying the mix of stocks and bonds, you'll get a different projection.

"Sound like it's much more accurate," Pat said.

It's much more. Then, the projections are expressed as probabilities. It will give you a 85% probability that your money will last the rest of your life, for instance, depending on the inputs. If you change the inputs…say you delay retiring by three years, then the probabilities will change too. Maybe they go to a 95% chance of not running out of money.

For instance, it can show you that during a 25-year retirement period if you have 80% stock and 20% bonds in your retirement funds and you try to withdraw 5% for income each year, you have only a 77% probability that your money will last. Or, if you take 4% a year, your probability of success rises to 91%." You decide what's comfortable for your situation. You can get charts and Monte Carlo models from T. Rowe Price, one of the larger, good companies out there who are offering retirement help to people. Their web site is at www.troweprice.com and you can find all kinds of tools to help you decide if you can retire.

A Monte Carlo analysis can answer the following, important questions for every person looking at retirement:

1. Can I reach my goal, or can I reach multiple goals (retirement and college funding for grandchildren) and what are the chances of success? (Probability of success)

2. How will different strategies affect my success? (If I alter the contributions I make while working, delay retirement, take more risk in the retirement portfolio)

3. How can I make the best use of Asset Allocation? What types of investments should I put into my retirement funds?

4.   What percentage can I withdraw per year and retain a high probability of not running out of money before I die?

Asset Allocation

"We find our friend the Asset Allocation model again. Only this time, we answer the questions differently," I said.

"Like the one where it asks you how long it'll be before you need to start drawing money from your accounts? 'Cause we need the income now," Pat said.

"Right. The model will change a lot. It'll get more conservative. The idea is to try and remove as much volatility from your assets as possible. We can't control the market, of course, but we can put your eggs in different baskets to avoid the worst ups and downs. Like before, we want to rebalance each year."

Prior to retiring, investor's actually get help from the ups and downs of the market, the volatility of the market. This works because they can "dollar cost average" to take advantage of opportunities to buy low and sell high. Since they rebalance each year, the human emotions are removed from the decisions to invest and where to invest. But once a person retires, volatility becomes a big enemy. It works this way because now, the investor must take money out of their accounts. If the market is down and the investor continues to take out the same amount each month, it's easy to see they would start eating into the principal.

This is where an Asset Allocation model can help. By changing your answers to the questions for the model, it will automatically reallocate your investment choices to more conservative, steady funds that have much less volatility. It serves to protect you more from the ups and downs, even if you're drawing money out. It will serve to minimize a person's losses, and reduce risk. For people in their retirement years, who are taking money out of their investments, this aspect is critically important. Monte Carlo analysis and Asset Allocation modeling give the investor some powerful tools to successfully make their money last.

Boost Savings and Emergency Money

As you get older, it makes sense to add to your cash savings. Something you can get your hands on right away if you need to. For instance, it's not a dumb idea to sock–away a full year's living expenses, or even two years.

"Sure, I see. Then, if the market drops, you don't have to sell your investments, you can simply draw from your savings until the market comes back," Charlie said.

"But remember Charlie, in any down market, not <u>everything</u> is going down. You could draw from your investments but only from those that had risen in value. Use your savings to supplement whatever you're able to take from investments. Wait until the market's back up again."

Pat added, "Then build-up your savings again with money you take from investment accounts. So, it goes back to something you told us weeks ago. To try and delay taking money out of the investment accounts."

Immediate Annuities

Depending on your situation, you could invest in an Immediate Annuity. It's a simple process with a funny name. We've brought up annuities before, but here's an example of two people I worked with last month.

Dana and Ron both retired from private employers and each had a 401(K) as their primary retirement savings. As a result, every time the market dropped, they worried about their money running out. They tried to use a savings account, but this couple was still worried. I was too because they really didn't have a lot saved and they retired early. When the market went up, they lived well. But when it dropped, they went back to eating peanut butter sandwiches for dinner. It was very stressful.

I suggested they take about 25% of their funds and buy an immediate annuity. The process is simple: they gave the 25% cash to an insurance company I had selected that agreed to good terms for Dana and Ron. In return for the money, the insurance company guaranteed to pay them a fixed, monthly amount for the rest of their lives. They could count on this amount regardless of what the market did. When the market went down, they relied more upon the annuity payments and left their investments to weather the downturn.

This doesn't work for everyone but when it does, it's really great. There are more uses for Immediate Annuities that will be explored later.

Delay Taking Social Security

One final idea is to delay taking your Social Security benefits. Of course, by doing this, you'll get a larger amount so that you may not have to draw as much from your investments in the future. For instance, by waiting from 62 until 66, your benefit will go up by approximately 25–27%. What happens is that you trade four years of no payments, for twenty-plus years of higher payments, if you live into your late 80's. If you can cover your living expenses from 62 to 66 without taking much out of your retirement accounts, this is a great idea.

Basically, it enables you to have a higher income from the government, so you don't need to take as much income from your investments, particularly when the markets are down. You can weather these drops because you've got a larger income to live on while you wait for the markets to rise in value. Then, as the values of your investments go up, you can began drawing from your them again.

What my notes said

1. Although most of us would like to see the stock market rise all the time, that's not going to happen, Instead, while a person is working, there are ways to take advantage of the ups and downs of the market.

2. I showed Charlie and Pat that some of the tools they used before like Asset Allocation models would help them and, while they're contributing to their accounts, they should practice dollar-cost averaging to actually buy stocks at a low, average price.

3. Volatility is a friend when you're contributing to investment plans. Once we retire, this becomes, along with inflation, one of our worst enemies. Strategies to minimize this include Asset Allocation models and an emergency fund of cash to use during down markets. Minimizing losses is critically important to the long-term health of your accounts.

4. I introduced the powerful tool of Monte Carlo modeling to use in predicting the probabilities of running out of money before they die. The answer to this will give them insight into the use of strategies to make their money last.

5. Immediate annuities can be helpful to protect against the ups and downs of the market because an insurance company promises to pay a monthly amount for the rest of your life, regardless of what happens in the market.

6. A delay in taking Social Security benefits, if you can afford it, means a higher income for the rest of your lives, too. In down markets, you may have enough income from Social Security to avoid using your retirement money.

Lesson Four:
Learn to get your <u>money working harder</u> for your, rather than <u>you working harder</u> for your money

Lesson Four:
Learn to get your <u>money working harder</u> for you, rather than <u>you working harder</u> for your money

Chapter Eight

Your money and it's hard work become your new partner

Spring rolled along toward summer, bringing rain. Clouds covered the landscape in Minnesota. Billowing elms and Lindens had enough leaves now that the wind could catch them and bend them to its direction. Lilac bushes decorated hundreds of back yards, spreading their perfume in the air like an oil drop on water. Kingfishers, thrashers, martins, and bluebirds returned from their sun country vacations. They worked hard to build nests and find their mates. You could hear how hard they worked from the songs they called to each other. The air smelled dense, moist, rich, and pregnant.

Many people constantly wonder if they were doing the right things with their money. There is so much talk, usually called "advice", that it's easy to become confused. Especially when people stopped working, they want to make sure their money is working as hard as it could. It always seemed that other people made "killings" in their investments. Why couldn't we? the rest of us wonder.

I met Charlie and Pat at the door to the waiting room. I offered good coffee or water, as usual. "Welcome. Where were we when we left off?"

"Working," Charlie said. "You encouraged us not to."

"Oh, yeah. Well, I didn't mean that literally," I chuckled. "But you need muscle in your money. You gotta get your assets working hard, make them more powerful."

Almost always, people need to rearrange their money once they quit working. At that time, working for income shifts from each person and their jobs, to money. Now, it has to work to produce their income. And those dollars may as well work as hard as possible for them. There's no secret investment I'd recommend, but it's important to get your investments "powered-up".

Your money is your new business

First, you have to change your way of thinking. Most people work and save their money in retirement funds, hoping for the best. You have to begin thinking of your investments as your very own business. And your dollars are the employees, working for you. But unlike people, you can work them as hard as possible without having to give them a break. They work 24 hours a day and can keep working for many generations. It's a different way of looking at money. All of your dollars should be included in the new job description.

Actually, people usually ignore most of their dollars. They have no idea where the dollars are or what they're doing. Maybe people are afraid of their money. It's a fundamental shift, to move from thinking of your money as a storehouse of value locked away somewhere, to active management of them. You hope that when you open the doors to that locked room, the value of your dollars will have grown magically. The shift to thinking of your money as active participants in your retirement is tough. You have to view them in place of yourself, working every morning, just like you. You control them. You have the choice to employ them to their fullest. Here are some ideas.

Money Market funds

"Remember we talked about having an emergency fund? Most people, if they save anything at all, leave it in checking or a savings account. There are better places."

"Like CD's?" Pat said.

They're good and lots of people use them. Usually, these are purchased for a set period of time. If you don't need them, that's fine. And, they're insured by the

FDIC at a bank. But if you face an emergency and need your dollars, you may have to sacrifice some of the interest you've earned to cash them in. Money market funds work better.

They're really mutual funds, which lots of people don't realize. But unlike other funds where the value of the shares go up and down, money market funds are priced at one dollar a share. What changes is the growth rate. And that rate tends to follow the Federal Reserve Board's raising and lowering of interest rates.

"That's why right now, those pay only one or two percent." Pat said.

"Yeah. But do you remember that in the late 90's they were paying 5 ½ percent? Or the greatest example was in the late seventies. They were paying around 14 percent! Of course, home mortgage rates were at 18 percent then," I said.

Five and a half percent's not too far out of the averages. If you had $50,000 in your emergency fund in money markets, that would grow about $2,750 for the year.

You won't get rich on this rate, but these little advantages add up.

Shelter Severance pay as much as possible

"Let me tell you a story about Betty, a client who left teaching after thirty-two years. Like many employees, she received a severance payment when she quit. Let's look at her numbers."

She's going to get $35,000 from her accumulated sick leave and vacation time that she's never used. Betty's husband is still working and brings in $80,000 a year. Betty could simply take the money, run, and pay taxes. But if she did, she could give-up as much as $10,000. We checked with her employer, who had a deferred compensation program. It's much like a 401(K). Anyway, she was able to put $18,000 of her severance pay into deferred comp. That left only $17,000 of taxable income.

"Did they file a joint tax return?" Pat said. "Could her husband put $17,000 of his salary into his 401(K) while they lived on her $17,000? Wouldn't that have the effect of sheltering all of her severance pay?"

That's exactly what Betty said, too. Once she got the idea of avoiding taxes to get her money working harder, she came up with all kinds of great ideas! Most employers have similar opportunities for employees who are retiring. People quitting should take advantage of these things.

Saving taxes is always a way to put more money into your pocket and, therefore, have the opportunity to invest it to work harder for you.

Roll-overs of Retirement Dollars

I said, "Speaking of retirement money, when you leave your employment, you should 'roll-over' the funds into a self-directed IRA."

"What's a roll-over?"

It's a IRS term that allows you to move money from one retirement vehicle to another without paying any taxes or penalties. So, if you've got money in a 401(K), deferred compensation, TSA, or other retirement plans, once you quit working, you can move it to another retirement plan. The tax treatment will be the same. There are three big reasons to move your money and few, if any, not to move it.

1.   **Reduced Fees**

     Besides the fees you pay to the mutual fund companies in the plan (which you'll still pay in a self-directed IRA), there are administrative fees that you don't even know you're paying. Under federal law, an employer must use a third party to handle the retirement program. The employer and third party contract to set-up and administer a retirement program, like a TSA. The Third Party Company charges an administrative fee to the employer which often gets passed on to the employees. While you're working, it's okay and frankly, you can't get out of it anyway. But after you quit, you don't need to pay that fee. It can be quite hefty. In a self-directed IRA, since you manage the plan, there should be little or no administrative fees. (You will still probably have to pay a small administrative fee to the mutual funds for their operation.)

2.   **Freedom of choice**

     Most of these plans have very limited distribution or withdrawal options. Some, like the 457 deferred comp plans, can be limited to a few choices. And once you make the choice, you're stuck in concrete for the rest of your life. With an IRA, the choices are limitless.

3.   An IRA is the best way for your children or beneficiaries to **inherit** your retirement money. The ease and freedoms of this post death transfer are incredible. Your beneficiaries will also have the opportunity to "stretch" the required minimum distributions over their entire lifetime. Meaning,

your money could continue to grow and work hard long after you're gone.

I told them a story of an employee of a local county government, who was client of mine.

Bill, the client, had about $100,000 in deferred compensation plans. He wanted to take it out before he turned 65. When he checked, he was limited to taking all the money out over either a five-year period or a ten-year period. Under the five-year distribution that meant he'd get $20,000 a year for five years whether he needed that much or not. Of course, he'd have to pay full tax on all of the $20,000.

I advised him to roll-over the $100,000 to an IRA. Until he hit his 70 ½ birthday and triggered the Required Minimum Distribution rules, Bill could take out as much or as little as he wanted every year. He had complete freedom of choice. When he died, his wife could inherit it and when she died, it could go to his children. That $100,000 had the possibility of growing for years and years. A good example of Bill choosing to get his money working harder for him.

When you look at 401(K)'s the case is even better to roll-over your money.

Sometimes, the plan will force you to take out all the money as quickly as five years after you quit. Whether you need it or not and regardless of whether your tax bracket can handle the extra income. Here's another story...a horror story.

Years ago, I was teaching a class in money management for people who were in between jobs. When I got to this subject, everyone appreciated the information. One older gentleman met me at the break near the coffeepot. Steve Maxwell was his name. He told me he'd actually moved through six different employers in the past twenty years—something very common now. Along the way, he'd never known to rollover his 401(K) money from each former employer. Seems that a larger company had acquired the second employer. The third one had gone bankrupt. When Steve tried to find out about the two 401(K)'s years later, he couldn't find out anything! They had disappeared.

"There are laws that protect the employees' money in those," I said. "But he still couldn't find the money. Even if the law is there, it'll take him years to sue and recover his money...if he can."

"I guess for me," Pat said, "it's simple. I want control of my own money as soon as I can get my hands on it. I don't trust all these employers. You read all these stories about so many companies under funding their retirement plans—even though the law says they're not supposed to."

"I agree. There have been very few times when I could see any reason to leave the money in the employer's retirement plan. Of course, I'm not talking about pensions or defined benefit plans. That's a whole different ball game. I'm talking about defined contribution plans."

Lease or buy a car?

"This is a question that I get all the time," I said. "It was never a problem when cars cost $15,000. And it's a good idea not to buy a new car. A car loses one-third of its value the first year. But I've got a heck of a lot of clients who are buying $35,000 to $45,000 cars or even more expensive."

Let's look at the numbers again. Many retired people have access to enough money to be able to pay cash for their cars. But look what they've done. Forty thousand dollars are tied-up in something they can't get an income from and really, is losing money for them!

"How about financing?" Pat asked.

"Then they end up paying even more for the car...fifty-five, sixty thousand. That's a lot of money to put into something that can't possibly earn anything for you. With the price of cars now, it makes sense to lease the same car. But..." I raised my finger in the air. "That also means they should invest the difference."

"What do you mean?"

"If you can afford to pay cash for it, lease the car instead and invest the cash. It wouldn't be too hard to generate an income of about $150 a month from a $40,000 investment. And, in the end, you still have your $40,000. The $150 could be used to help make your lease payments."

"And if they're financing?" Pat said.

"The lease payments should be a lot less. Invest the difference between the financing cost and the lease payments. At the end of five or six years, you'd have a nice pile of money."

"This wouldn't make as much sense for cheaper cars, would it?"

"Nope. I don't think so." I tapped the end of my pen against the yellow pad. "With those opportunities, if you can afford to pay cash for the purchase price, do so. Perhaps, the best way to buy a car is to look for one a year or two old. That way, most of the early depreciation is already gone and priced out of the car. Then, drive that care for 200,000 miles! In the long run, this is the cheapest way to own. People complain that the repair costs are 'killing them'. But those costs are really a lot less than the cost of a new car, including depreciation, which we don't see as a cash expense. Of course, many of us don't want to drive old cars that far."

Apply your Asset Allocation model to all your investments

"We talked about the benefits of following your asset allocation model for your retirement funds. It's important to apply it to everything you own. Like…if you have cash value insurance, annuities, stocks and bonds, real estate. Everything should fit into the model to make sure you're getting the most out of your investments."

"So, we should look at each investment and follow the pie-shaped chart? What if the investment doesn't offer the types of funds we need?" Pat said.

You could apply the model across everything. Let's look at Betty again. As a retired schoolteacher, she has a nice pension from the state that pays her a guaranteed monthly income for the rest of her life. It's even indexed to keep up with the cost of inflation. Let's suppose her model shows that she needs 20% of her assets in bonds or fixed income investments. I think she could count her pension as if it were a fixed income investment. It acts the same way, after all, by paying a regular, fixed amount each month. She could take a more aggressive position with the rest of her retirement money, knowing she had the security of the pension.

"It sounds like you really believe in Asset Allocation," Pat said.

"The unbiased academics have shown the power of this strategy. So yeah, I think it's one of the most important tools we can use to get our money working for us. You know, Betty's situation reminds me of another idea."

Don't be too cautious early in your retirement

"I don't know..," Pat said. "I don't want to lose anything."

"'Course not. But here's what I see often if a couple retires in their late 50's. They've probably got almost thirty years left. Their money not only has to last, it must grow faster than inflation or they'll sink. I see lots of fifty year olds buying CD's after they retire because they're so worried about losing money."

"Oh, yeah. You mentioned something before about this," Pat said.

"Over seventy-five years of record keeping shows that stocks have <u>always</u> out-performed CD's on the average. By a huge margin. To start buying CD's is to settle for the little car rather than the powerful one. Of course, you balance all of this with your allocation model."

Pat said, "So you think the time to get more conservative in our investments is in our seventies?"

"Maybe eighties. After all Pat, a healthy woman of your age has a life expectancy of over ninety years! You've got a lot of living for your money to support and grow. You folks are further along in this process than many I work with. But all of us need to be challenged. Attitude leads to all success."

"What do you mean?"

"Well, we've been talking about viewing your money as an employee for you. Most people let money control them; they work for their money, not the other way around. In a larger sense, we all need to have an attitude that good and successful things will happen to us. But lots of times, it doesn't seem to work that way. Especially when people get older and have health problems, for instance," I said.

Try not to dwell on those negative things. You have to think about them long enough to try and solve them but then, try hard to revert to the positive, good things that are happening all around you. Purposely push the negative emotions in the background. Things like anger, jealousy, blame, resentment, self-pity. These sap us of all energy. Focusing on the positive and possible actually enable us to be open when these things come along.

"I try to do the same," said Pat, "but it's hard."

It's a daily effort. But the more you force yourself to get rid of the negative junk, the more it becomes a habit and then, it's easier. What's so critical about retirement is that it's a clear change. You can get rid of the old excuses why you didn't live more positively and freely. Since you now have the power to create your own thoughts and activities, you can focus on squeezing all the juice out of each day, making the most of it. Each day can become a precious adventure.

Don't "annuitize" too early

"That sounds like something my doctor might say to me!"

"This applies to people who have retirement plans and the option of annuitizing them."

"You mean converting them to a regular, monthly payment plan?" Pat said.

"Right. The retired person makes a decision to convert a chunk of cash in a retirement plan into a stream of monthly payments. Most of these are then guaranteed to flow for the rest of their life."

"What's so bad about that? Sounds good to me," Charlie said.

"At the right time, it's great. But remember, once they convert, the chunk of cash disappears. It'll never grow anymore. The problems start when someone make this choice early in their life, like fifties or sixties."

Pat nodded. As usual, she was way ahead of us. "You said the payments are guaranteed for life buy they never change?"

"Nope. They stay the same."

"Inflation." Pat announced to us.

I nodded. "You're getting the right attitude, Pat. You're starting to think differently than you did a few months ago. You're seeing how these things link together. As the payments remain level, inflation is tearing down the purchasing power of those dollars. If you're seventy-five, let's say, it's not too big a problem. But if you're fifty-five, you have to make it through another twenty years or more of the inflation. You won't have any protection against the rising price of gas and movies."

"Why do people choose it, then?" Pat said.

"Fear…worry. They like the guaranteed feature. They don't think about how long their money has to last. At the right time, it's a wise choice. Too early, it could lead to disaster. Remember the postage stamps. Prices will generally always rise."

What my notes said

1. I encouraged them that instead of working harder during their retirement, they should get their money working harder for them.

2. They could do that by moving their "emergency" money into tools like Money Market funds.

3. They should roll-over their retirement accounts from employers, after they decide to quit. The strategy is to move them into self-directed IRAs to cut expenses, give them the greatest freedom of choice, and to provide fabulous inheritance opportunities for their children.

4. We discussed the pros and cons of leasing versus buying a car and when it makes sense to do one or the other.

5. I reminded them to apply their Asset Allocation model to all their money resources.

6. I also warned them that if they had the opportunity to annuitize an insurance product, don't do it too early into their retirement because the dollars are fixed forever and won't increase to cover the loss in purchasing power due to inflation.

Chapter Nine

Now your money's working harder for you

Creative use of insurance

I stood again and moved to a credenza in the far corner of the office. Pulling open the drawer, my fingers walked through several files until I found those I needed. I lifted them out and peered at them. "Here…here they are." Back at the table, I dropped several thick files in front of them. "These are clients I've helped in the past. I've made some notes to remind myself of what we did. There's one thing all these have in common. They were all retired and in trouble…financially. Through the creative use of life insurance, all of them got what they wanted. You should learn these lessons in case you need them."

"I thought that as we got older, the need for life insurance dropped," Pat said. "I remember buying it when the kids were younger. In case something happened to either of us, our income could be replaced with insurance money."

As a person gets older, to an extent, you don't need as much…at least not for the same purposes. Your kids are grown and so have your other assets. But sometimes, insurance can really add horsepower to your situation. These couples demonstrate some very important ways to have your money working for you.

Couple #1

This is the classic case of a couple with under-powered assets. They had a $100,000 CD paying about $2,100 a year. They wanted more income but they also wanted to leave something for their children—the $100,000 the kids would get when the couple died. What to do?

The wife bought a single premium life insurance policy (Instead of paying a monthly premium, they invested one, large premium that paid-up for the rest of her life with no more premiums due). It cost her $35,000 to buy a life insurance policy with a $100,000 death benefit. With the remaining $65,000 she bought an immediate annuity. When they finished, here's what they had:

Death benefit for the children to inherit tax-free: $100,000

Income from the annuity, after tax: 4,100/yr.

I pointed out the numbers here weren't large but the idea worked well. Also, each person's situation will be different. Their health and age will determine how much insurance they can get and at what cost.

Lady #2

This woman also had a CD worth $250,000. Unlike the previous couple, this lady didn't need any income from the CD. And since she felt safe with it, she didn't want to disturb it. At the same time, her grandchildren had doubled in number. She was very concerned to be able to give them each enough money after she died. What to do?

Since she didn't need the income from the CD, I persuaded her to take $10,000 a year in cash from the CD and buy a permanent life insurance policy. Each year, she contributed to the cash value with an investment of $10,000. At her age and health, she was able to purchase a policy with a death benefit of $232,000.

End results:

Her CD was preserved in the full $250,000 value

She almost doubled the amount of money her grandchildren would inherit after she died with the addition of $232,000 in death benefits.

"I realize these may not all apply to your situation," I told them, "but in the future, these ideas might help. If nothing else, I want to teach you to start thinking in a different way, not only about life insurance but about your money. Be creative!"

Couple #3

This couple had an old, small life insurance policy. They had three children they wanted to leave more money for. The policy on the husband had a death benefit of only $35,000. When he bought it nineteen years earlier, it seemed like a lot. With inflation, it wouldn't go very far with the three kids. Their problem was how to add more death benefit since their incomes weren't enough to afford the high premiums at their ages.

Luckily, he had about $25,000 of cash value in the policy. (Cash value is the build-up of money within a permanent life insurance policy that grows tax deferred during the life of the owner.)

I had them take $23,000 out of the first policy (a non-taxable source of cash) and purchase a new policy on the wife, using a single premium. She was able to obtain a policy with a $100,000 death benefit.

They ended with:

The first policy was still in effect with a death benefit of $35,000

The new policy was in effect and fully paid for with a death benefit of $100,000.

Many people already have an old life insurance policy. For a lot of reasons, they don't need it anymore. Can they add any horsepower to their financial situation with these old policies?

"Before you go further, Colin," Pat said, "what's the difference between term and permanent? I understand term to be temporary insurance, rather then permanent. We have some of each, don't we, Charlie?" She turned to him and he nodded. She said, "I've always been confused about the two."

"Is one better than the other?" Charlie asked.

I removed my glasses and rubbed my eyebrows. "Good question. Most people don't know the difference. Here, let me show you something." I laid a piece of paper on top of the file and made two columns. "Easy way to remember: term is like renting an apartment, permanent is like buying a house."

Term Insurance	Permanent Insurance
1. Renting	Buying
2. Cheaper	More expensive
3. Ends when you quit paying	Lasts a lifetime
4. No build-up of equity	Equity builds-up during lifetime
5. No growth or investment opportunities	Has investment/growth opportunities
6. Only lasts for "term" (10,20 years)	Lasts a lifetime

"When you put it this way, who would ever buy term?" Pat asked.

One's not better than the other. They work in different situations. All group insurance from employers is term, for instance. It's cheaper. When the employee leaves, the company can quit paying. In your case, as I recall, we invested in both types of policies because it's important to have permanent insurance, but it gets so expensive at the high levels you needed, that we supplemented it with big term policies. That gave you a huge death benefit for the kids at a much lower price.

Selling your own life policy for big money

Couple #4

"This is a lesson in selling insurance, "I said. "But this couple, my clients, are doing the selling."

"Wait a minute," Pat said. "I seem to remember in the early 90"s...people who had AIDS and were terminally ill, sold policies for cash. Something about that wasn't fair...they got ripped-off."

"Good memory. Lots of people got taken. Investors included," I said. "It's a different package today."

"How does it work? Who'd want to buy a life insurance policy from me? There's no cash value in term policies so, who'd want to buy those?"

There's really about $2 billion worth of people willing to buy policies. And that's growing about 20% a year. The process is quite simple. An investor, usually an institution, buys the policy from you, names themselves as the beneficiary, and begins to make the premium payments. So what they get is a big death benefit when the insured dies, and the seller gets a lump of cash today. This only works when two things happen: the elderly person doesn't need life insurance coverage and doesn't want to pay the premiums anymore. If a person still needs coverage, don't do this! And the prices paid for these policies usually aren't worth much until the person gets more than 65.

"What kinds of numbers are we talkin' about?"

This is couple number four.

The wife didn't need her policy anymore but could use extra cash. A buyer paid about $250,000 for her $1 million term policy. She was 66. Then there was a client in his 80's that we sold a $2 million permanent policy with a cash value of about $54,000 to an investor for $232,000.

"For a term policy?" Pat said.

"Sure. People don't realize just how much value there really is in their old life policies. Typically, the policy sold must have at least a $200,000 death benefit. Investors won't look at anything much smaller."

"I see the benefit to getting assets working harder," Pat said. "Instead of sitting on the $54,000 cash value, the seller turned that into $232,000. Nice." She nodded.

"Yeah but then the 80-year old gave-up a $2 million death benefit for his heirs," Charlie said.

"Sure but that's his business, isn't it?" I said. "Besides, he had plenty of other assets so he didn't need the life insurance anymore. If a person has a permanent policy, we can usually get them at least three times the amount of cash they have in the policy. That's a great way to get your money working harder for you!"

"And now the consumer has a choice," Pat said.

Don't buy timeshares, cemetery plots, etc.

"I may have to get my microphone and amp out for this one," I said. "I can't say this loudly enough: don't buy timeshares or cemetery plots, or anything like these. There are lots of people pushing this stuff on the consumer, especially the elderly, and it doesn't make any sense." I slapped the table in front of them several times to emphasize each sentence.

"But we've got lots of friends who come back from vacation with a week or two of timesharing. They never appealed to me," Pat said, "but lots of people have 'em."

"Of course. And you know how most of these schemes are sold, don't you? Doesn't that tell you something right there?" I shook my head. "Let's look at the easiest one: cemetery plots. 'Buy one now before the price goes up and you can't afford it.' They tell old people. But how fast is the price of plots going up? Almost always, the person could get better growth in liquid investments than 'putting their money in the ground'!"

"Every time we're on vacation at the beach, we get hit by people trying to sell us time shares. I've heard them say buy now to permanently lock-in the cost of your vacation," Pat said.

Here's how they typically work. You make a down-payment that can run any-where from a few thousand dollars to twenty or thirty thousand. Then, you make monthly payments for taxes, insurance, maintenance, and management. Those costs, by the way, will definitely go up…fast! Let's not even talk about the quality of management you get. That can change every year and some are good, some are bad.

"But it's true that you lock-in the cost of the condo, for instance," Charlie said.

The real equation you have to look at, is to compare the growth in the <u>increased</u> cost of renting the condo every year versus the growth that twenty thousand dol-lars can get for you in another investment. There's no comparison. Economists estimate that even if you use your timeshare <u>every single year</u>, without skipping a year, it'll take you almost twenty years to break-even and begin to see the financial benefit of putting your money into it.

Pat said, "But some people just love a spot so much, they want the assurance they can keep coming back, keep affording it."

If they buy a timeshare for that reason, okay. But they shouldn't be fooled into thinking this is something that'll get their money working harder for them. It's not. It's an emotional decision. That's okay by me, if people truly understand the crimp they're putting on their money.

Analyze all these offers carefully. Almost always, your are trying to beat infla-tion in the cost of the thing you want, like rooms on a beach. Sometimes, infla-tion in certain products is higher than the consumer price index. Still, you can probably stay ahead of inflation with your investments, be able to afford these things in the future, and have money left over. Plus, you stay "liquid", which is a term that means you can have easy access to your cash if you need it for an emergency, for instance. If you tie up your money in a time share and have to keep paying monthly fees, your money is trapped in that place. By investing it somewhere else, you can get your money working harder for you.

Should we pay off the house?

"Wait a minute, Colin. I've got a question," Pat said. "I'm real confused about our house. Most of our friends say they'd like to pay off their homes when they retire. It's usually their largest asset. And it seems to make sense. I mean, if we could get rid of our mortgage payment, that'd free-up a lot of cash."

"Yeah. We've talked to lots of people who think that way," Charlie said. "From what you've been teaching us, about getting our money working harder, this could be a no-brainer. I've seen charts in magazines that show how much money you could save by paying off your mortgage as soon as possible. It can be hundreds of thousands. Instead of paying all that extra interest to the bank, we could use it."

I paused and smiled. "That's probably the question I get most often. And it depends…There's no right answer." I paused when their faces screwed up. "It's a left brain, right brain kind of an answer."

I propped the green pen behind my ear. "You know about the left brain? Supposedly, it makes all our rational, logical, analytical decisions for us. And the right side," I raised my right hand toward my ear, "makes the emotional, intuitive, creative decisions."

I pulled the green pen off my ear and wrote at the top of a yellow pad with a line drawn down the middle.

Left Brain   Right Brain

"Let's look at the reasons for both." I turned to Pat. "If you wanted to pay off the house, <u>why</u> would you do it?"

"I'm not sure I want to," said Pat. "Well…I remember my Grandma. She and Grandpa had four kids during the Depression but managed to save a little every month so that by the time they were in their forties, they were finally able to buy a nice home. Their first one." She paused. "Little different than people today who want to buy a home, a big one, right out of college. Anyway, they bought it and by their seventies, they'd paid it all off. I remember sitting with my relatives, drinking weak 'grandma coffee', and listening to the adults. Starting with the grandparents, they all agreed that that house was sacred. They never borrowed against it all their lives. Could you imagine her reaction to all these home equity loans today? And they never entirely trusted banks. 'Pay it off. Don't owe anybody nothing'…but I don't know. Things've changed."

I wrote on the right side of the paper.

Left Brain	Right Brain
	Grandma said so

"That's exactly what I mean. Your memory Pat, provides an emotional reason to pay off the mortgage. It's powerful, isn't it?"

"Yeah, now that you mention it. But is it right for us?"

If you feel better with the idea of paying it off or if you can't sleep at night until it's paid-off, then, pay it off. That becomes the "correct" answer for you. Whether it makes analytical financial sense is irrelevant. Because your emotional decisions are equally valid with the logical ones. I know this reason I wrote sounds funny to us sitting here. But believe me, lots of my clients feel this way. They're kind of embarrassed and won't tell me, but they have reasons like this. For them, they should pay it off.

"So we don't always have to do the logical, analytical thing?" Charlie asked.

"I think when I show you the logical reasons not to pay it off, the emotional ones will disappear. But whatever…either choice can be a good one depending on the circumstances."

Left Brain	Right Brain
True cost of money is less than you think	Grandma said so

"Pat, let's look at those numbers you found in the magazine article. I can put some numbers here." Inside my briefcase was a calculator. I retrieved it and set it on top of the yellow pad. "Let's see…if we have a…" On a new sheet of paper, I wrote.

Purchase price of new home	$350,000
Less 20% down payment	-70,000
Mortgage balance	280,000
Payment 6.5% interest for 30 yrs.	$1,770/month

$1,770 for 12 months for 30 years=Total amount principal+interest = $637,200

It's really not as much as it looks. This is a very simple analysis and because it's so simple, it's very inaccurate. It's not the "true cost" of the house. For one thing, look at the interest rate. Are you really paying 6.5%?

Back went the green pen to the new paper.

Interest rate on loan	6.5%
Less tax savings (30%)	-1.95
Net rate	4.55%

Since you're deducting your interest payments from your income, you folks are in the marginal tax rate, federal and state, of about 30%. That means for every dollar you pay in interest, you save 30 cents in taxes.

"I get it," Pat said. "Because of the deduction of interest, we're really paying less. Cash goes out for the mortgage payment, but we get back some in saved taxes we don't have to pay."

It gets better.

Net rate	4.55%
Less inflation	-3.10%
New net rate	1.45%

Because you have a fixed payment each month, inflation becomes a friend to you, for once. Each year, the dollars you pay are worth a little less. So that's what you're paying to borrow $280,000–1.45%. Pretty cheap, huh? It's almost free money!

"When you said the first example of paying $637,200 out in thirty years was too simplified, I see what you meant. We'll pay that in cash out of pocket, but when you analyze it, the true cost was much less. Wait a minute!" Charlie said. "Why don't we take out the biggest mortgage, buy the biggest house we can if borrowing money is really so cheap?"

"Good question. Be careful because you still have to afford the monthly payment today. And, that leads to another point on the left side," I said.

Left Brain	Right Brain
True cost of money is less than you think	Grandma said so
Growth rates aren't as good as they seem	

"What would you say if I told you your house wasn't a good investment?" I said.

"I'd really question that," Pat said. "We've got friend who bought their homes for a $100,000 and twenty years later, are selling them for $400,000. What's wrong with that?"

Your house is a great place to live and you've lived rent-free for years. But it's not a good investment. Let's look at a couple of things. In the past sixty years or so, housing has grown about 4%–5% a year on the average. Oh…I know there are spikes in prices, like the so-called "housing bubble" we see in some parts of the country. But for the most part, the growth's been modest. During the same period, the stock market grew about 10% on the average.

"Okay," Pat said finally, "but you can't argue with the profit people are making on the sale of their houses."

Look at an example.

Couple buys the house for $100,000 and sells twenty years later for $400,000. A simplistic look at this seems to show they've got a profit of $300,000. But you're forgetting all the money they spent on the house during those twenty years: mortgage payments, insurance, taxes, repairs, upkeep, improvements, utilities, equipment like lawnmowers and snow lowers, lawn care, paint, all the tools you need. If they kept accurate records of all these expenses, your friends might've actually spent <u>more</u> than $300,000 over twenty years!

"I've never thought of home ownership like this," Charlie said. "Well then, why do we even own a house if it's such a bad deal?"

I wrote again.

<u>Left Brain</u>	<u>Right Brain</u>
True cost of money is less than you think	Grandma said so
Growth rates aren't as good as they seem	
You live rent free	

If your friends only break-even after twenty years and get all the money they put into the house back out again, then they lived in a nice place "for free". That's a good deal but not a good reason to pay off the house. Here's one last idea.

<u>Left Brain</u>	<u>Right Brain</u>
True cost of money is less than you think	Grandma said so
Growth rates aren't as good as they seem	
Live rent free	
Largest asset locked in "handcuffs"	

For most people, the equity in their house is the largest asset they have. But we've seen that it's not working very hard for them. Remember our lessons on asset allocation. For lots of people, a huge chunk of their net worth's in their home and isn't balanced with an equal amount of stocks, bonds, or mutual funds. The other problem is what economists call "liquidity". If you need money for an emergency, you can't sell a window or a garage to raise the cash. If you borrow, you're doing exactly what you didn't want to do if you paid-off your mortgage.

Pat said, "Lemme see if I get this. We shouldn't pay off the mortgage and with the extra money we have, we should invest it outside of the house?"

"If you can afford to pay extra on your mortgage, don't. Put it into a Roth IRA, for instance, or other investments."

"But then we're stuck with a mortgage payment at seventy years old!" she said.

It's a simple trade off. The money you've invested outside your home has grown on its own. Now, at seventy, if you need it, you can take part of it and pay off whatever's left on the mortgage. A better idea is to start drawing an income off that investment that <u>will pay the mortgage for you.</u>

"It always sounds so simple when you explain it," Pat said. "Maybe Grandma's advice isn't the best for us."

My notes said

1. In order to maximize the work of your money, there are several creative uses for insurance that will "power-up" cash that you may already have that's sitting in idle places.

2. Avoid investments in time shares, cemetery plots, etc. because they tie up your money in something that's probably not growing much, if any. There are more productive uses for you money, where it'll grow so that when you need a vacation place on the beach, you can afford to rent it.

3. It seldom "pays" to pay off your house early unless there is an emotional or sentimental reason to do so. Whether the reason is logical or emotional, both choices were okay–depending on the individual.

Chapter Ten

Sources of Income

I work with many clients who are thinking of retiring or have already retired. Many of the things I counsel them to consider are new to them. Usually, people plan for a year or two in advance. Let's face it. It's hard to think about what might happen ten years from now. Unlike other generations that quit working, the Baby Boom generation is different. Many of the rules that people followed before have changed. The importance of this hit me hard when I read a book by Robert C. Carlson, called The New Rules of Retirement, 2005.

The author has written alarmingly about the "Age Wave" that's washing into our midst: "A force that is bigger than anything that has tested retirement plans so far is causing these changes (in retirement ideas). This force is coming. You cannot stop it. Neither can the government. The previous generation may have been the greatest generation but they were lucky too. They benefitted from low inflation, rising home values, the largest growth of pension coverage in the history of the country, medical miracles, growth of Social Security benefits, long life, and a robust postwar economy. Retirement issues for this generation were unusually simple. With their health and money, they flooded the southern parts of the country to enjoy themselves.

Their children face a far different, bleak outlook. The Baby Boomers make up the Age Wave that will obliterate many of the assumptions and models we used for retirement. Why? Their numbers, for one thing. The stress these numbers will put on government services, housing, and medical care is daunting. Combined with projected slower economic growth, higher inflation, crumbling home values, the almost total disappearance of the traditional pension, and reduction in Social Security and Medicare benefits, this new generation has got a lot of work cut out for it.

New models of life in retirement need to be developed. Not only financial models but also ones to include new activities, longer work lives, families, and even spiritual models need to change for these folks.

Studies show that less than 3% of Americans plan for their retirement and almost no one plans for afterward. What will they do for their long, remaining lives?

I think Robert Carlson is onto something important. Not only will the rules for people's money change, the rules for a fulfilling life may change also.

A few weeks later, we agreed to meet at a local Thai restaurant called "Thai One," an Asian restaurant that Charlie and Pat liked.

They selected it and frankly, I could understand why when we arrived. Besides the goofy name, the restaurant itself was located in a converted fast food place. I could see where the original counters had been from the marks on the tile floor. It probably hadn't been painted since the conversion. We walked in to noise and motion. The prices on the menu looked cheap. But it smelled great.

After ordering and pouring green tea for all of us, Charlie pulled himself up to the table. He wore tan khaki, wrinkled pants and a golf shirt, which strained to fit around his chubby middle. He must've been in the sun recently because his skin glowed a healthy pink.

I announced to them that although we'd spent a lot of time on the problems they'd face, today, we were going to learn some positive things. "Always a lot more fun." I dipped a spring roll in the mustard sauce, covering it completely.

"I can't wait to hear how I can make some extra income," said Pat. "We can always use more."

"We'll look to traditional sources first then go on to other, newer sources. A lot of the territory you're headed into is uncharted and you've got be prepared to use many resources in the future. Let's start with the three main ways people get income during retirement: **Pension** money, **Social Security** benefits, and **IRA** funds."

Traditional Pension Benefits

The sad news is that pensions are like the dinosaurs—they're disappearing fast. Today, only about 20% of retirees can count on a pension and that number's dropping. They're too expensive. Look at General Motors and many of the large airlines. They're in financial trouble, to a great degree, because they have to fund huge pensions and don't have the money to do it. A "pension" is often called a Defined Benefit plan.

"Where the retirement benefit is fixed?" Pat said.

The employer puts money into the fund during the working years and the employee usually contributes too. When they retire, there is a formula based on years of work and age that will tell you exactly what your monthly benefit will be. That's where the name 'defined benefit' comes in. The employer "guarantees" to pay the defined amount for the remainder of the retired person's life—-usually. Unless, the pension has been under funded, as is becoming more common.

"I've got friends in the county government office who talk about their Rule of Ninety," Charlie said.

That's a combination of their age and years of service. When those numbers add up to ninety, they're eligible to retire and collect a full pension benefit. These plans are disappearing because the employer takes all the risk—meaning that within the pension plan, money is invested in anticipation of being paid out later. If the market turns down on the investments, the employer still has to pay the full benefit to the retiree. That makes it very expensive and, in some ways unpredictable, for the employer. This explains why these plans are decreasing in popularity. Employers don't like to have these long term liabilities hanging around their necks. General Motors, for instance, obligated by contracts entered into years ago, now finds itself on the hook to pay millions in pension benefits it didn't plan on paying.

"I've got a small pension from the years I taught," Pat said. "It's called the Teachers Retirement Association."

"Perfect example for us to use. Most of these plans have an optimum time to retire to get the best benefit. They usually offer counseling to pre-retirees that you should take advantage of. Once you've chosen that, the next question that arises is whether to take a full benefit or partial, leaving some of it for a surviving spouse."

"In mine, for instance, I can take 100% of the money each month and leave nothing to Charlie if I die before him. Or, I can take a reduced benefit and leave Charlie 25% of my benefit, 50%, or 100%," said Pat. "I don't know which one to choose."

Pat brought out her last monthly Statement of Benefits from TRA.

TRA Statement of Benefits

Rule of 90 First Eligible   Average Monthly Salary Used
Formula Used: Step Rate= 48.98%

Benefit Options	Monthly Income During Your Life	Spouse's Monthly Income After Your Death
Single-life Benefit	$2,400	$0
25% Option	$2,000	$500
50% Option	$1,600	$800
75% Option	$1,200	$900

"So far, this is simple," Charlie said. "If we take the 25% option for instance, Pat will get $2,000 a month for the rest of her life. If she dies before me, the $2,000 stops but I get $500 a month for the rest of my life. We get that part. But which one should we choose?"

There are three things to consider.

1. Does the spouse have a substantial retirement source of money? Either their own pension or a large IRA/401(K). If so, the spouse may not need any of the TRA pension money and you could choose the largest benefit of the single life.

2. Does the couple have other, large assets? If they have lots of other money that could be used to fund retirement, the spouse may not need any of the TRA pension money and again, choose the single life.

3. If the couple doesn't have either of the above additional resources, then you move to an analysis called **Pension Maximization**.

Maximizing Pension Income

"Do you remember the Woody Allen film," I said, "called <u>Bananas</u>? The American is captured in a Latin American country and he's tortured by throwing him into a pit with a life insurance salesman!" I chuckled at the memory. "Well, these options in a pension plan are really about insurance."

"Because Charlie will get a monthly amount if I die, it acts like life insurance," said Pat. "And the cost of that 'insurance' is the difference in your monthly benefit. Here, look at my chart. For Charlie to get a $500 a month benefit, I have to give-up $400 a month during my life. That's the cost I 'pay' to insure my life."

"Got it. Now what?"

"Well, what if we could find a life insurance policy on you Pat, that would provide a $500 a month income for Charlie that cost **less** than $400 a month?"

"We should buy it because it's cheaper than the reduced benefit to me."

This doesn't always work and the person getting the pension might actually be better off "buying their insurance" through the pension plan. In your case, we'd have to find out the cost of a policy, figure out how much of a death benefit we need to create an income of $500, and the length of the policy.

Ideally she would look at permanent life insurance, but as you age, it becomes very expensive. On the other hand, if we could find 20-year term insurance, it'll run-out obviously. But by that time, your other assets will have grown so that other resources could provide the $500 a month to Charlie.

"So it's a matter of comparing the cost of an insurance policy to the cost of the reduced pension benefit?"

"It's a simple process but you'd be surprised that most people don't know anything about it. And my experience with the pension plan counselors is that they never mention it either."

The other, major concern is **inflation protection.** A consulting group named Hewitt Associates in Lincolnshire, Illinois, found that 98% of pensions are **not** indexed for inflation! To some degree not having a provision in your pension that automatically raises your benefits to keep up with inflation, can be offset with Social Security, because those benefits are indexed for inflation. Remember the example of the postage stamps. Inflation is a huge problem for all retired people.

The other strategy is to "dial-up" your other investments, in IRA's, for instance. Make your fund selection more aggressive to help you beat inflation. And if you remember your Asset Allocation model, you could use your pension income to "replace" the fixed-income percentage. Another idea is to save some of your pension benefits in the early years of your retirement to build-up your nest egg in other investments that can beat inflation.

We looked up as the young, thin Thai waitress brought heaping plates of food to the table. She set the Pad Thai in front of Charlie. His eyes lit up and he attacked the plate with gusto. First he mixed the noodles around then he squeezed several lemons over the plate.

After we had eaten for a while, Charlie asked me, " I hear lots of my colleagues at the company, arguing about when to take Social Security. At 62 or at 66? Which do you recommend?"

"I get the same question every single day. Most people are very confused about it. By the way, you know you could wait until 70 to take Social Security, don't you?"

"No. Why would anyone wait that long?"

"Lots of good reasons. But let's back up first."

Maximizing Social Security Benefits

Social Security benefits are another asset you have. So they can be managed to get the biggest value. The program offers options that can increase or reduce your benefits. And remember, benefits can be taxed now. When you retire, your benefit is calculated on your highest thirty-five years of earnings. There's something called you "full retirement age", which changes, depending on when you were born. For instance, if you were born between 1943 and 1954, your age would be sixty-six.. After that, the full retirement age is sixty-six plus two months. Here's a chart from the Social Security Administration.

	Benefit Reductions for Early Retirement			
Year of Birth	Full Retirement Age	Age 62 Reduction Months	Monthly % Reduction	Total % Reduction
1937 or earlier	65	36	.555	20.00
1938	65 + 2 mo.	38	.548	20.83
1939	65 + 4 mo.	40	.541	21.67
1940	65 + 6 mo.	42	.535	22.50
1941	65 + 8 mo.	44	.530	22.33
1942	65 + 10 mo.	46	.525	24.17
1943-1954	66	48	.520	25.00
1955	66 + 2 mo.	50	.516	25.84
1956	66 + 2 mo.	52	.512	26.66
1957	66 + 2 mo.	54	.509	27.50
1958	66 + 2 mo.	56	.505	28.33
1959	66 + 2 mo.	58	.502	29.17
1960 and after	67	60	.500	30.00

I pointed my finger at the Year of Birth 1934–1954. "Here you are. And, of course, you are also eligible for the reduced income benefit at age sixty-two. If you look on the second column from the left, it shows you what percentage reduction the early age will cost you. By the way, the Social Security web site is a good place to get more information. It's at www.ssa.gov. What I'd like to spend our time on, are the strategies that you can use to get the most out of the program. The easiest way to start is to calculate your break-even point."

"You mean between taking it at sixty-two versus taking it at sixty-six?" Charlie said.

"It's actually very easy. Here are the numbers from a client I just worked with. I can't tell you the real name, so let's call her Betty."

Pat interrupted, "Wouldn't it be better to take the early benefit because you'd collect the money for four extra years, even thought the dollar amount is reduced?"

"There are some people who retire and absolutely need their Social Security money to live on. For those, of course, take it as soon as you can. But for the rest who don't need the money immediately to survive, we need to calculate the break-even point." I drew out the green pen again and flipped over the chart. On the backside I wrote.

Calculate the break-even point

Betty's present age: 62

Betty's Full Retirement Benefit at 66 $1,600/month

Betty's Reduced Benefit at 62 (75% of the Full) $1,200/month

If Betty takes the money at sixty-two, she will receive $1,200 a month for an extra forty eight months until she reaches age sixty-six..

$1,200 times 48 = $57,600 Total benefits received by Age 66

Divide $57,600 by the extra monthly amount, $400 = 144 months.

This demonstrates that it will take Betty 144 months to make up for waiting until the normal retirement age or sixty-six. Or, to make it easier, she'll have to live 144 months longer, to about age seventy-eight, to break-even.

"Meaning, at seventy eight, she'll have collected the same either way?" Pat said.

"Sure. If she lives longer than this, she'd get more than if she had waited to collect until age 66 because she'd be getting $1,600 a month from age 74 for the rest of her life."

"That doesn't seem very old," Pat said.

"No. But since the 1980's the charts were set-up so that everyone breaks-even if they live to their normal life expectancy. In Betty's case, age 78."

"But most people live far longer than that," Charlie said.

"Not so fast, Charlie. I've got some clients with serious illnesses who, unfortunately, don't think they'll get there. For them, the choice is simple: take it as soon as you can. Or if you've got a family history of early deaths, might be a good idea to take the money and run."

"Well, in our case we're healthy and we don't need the extra income right away…I don't know. It's still a tough choice," Charlie said.

There are other factors to consider that may help.

Inflation indexing and Investment possibilities

Since the benefits are indexed for inflation, which we didn't use in this example, when you go through a period of high inflation, your break-even age gets pushed out further. In Betty's case to, maybe, age eighty or eighty-one. Will she live that long? If you can afford to delay taking the benefits until age sixty-six, why not take them at sixty-two and invest the money somewhere else to be used later. Again, as this separate investment account grows, it has the effect of pushing out the break-even point.

"What do most people do?"

"Statistics from the feds show us that 41.6% of men and 52.2% of women take their benefit at age sixty-two. Quite a few. I personally think it's because most people fear they might die before collecting much in benefits. They figure that since they've paid into Social Security for years, they better darn well get something out of it!"

Penalties from Working

Age	Annual Allowance Before penalty is assessed	Penalty
Prior to year full Retirement is reached	$12,000	$1.00 for each $2.00 earned Above the Allowance
Year full retirement Is reached	$31,800	$1.00 for each $3.00 earned Above the Allowance
Years after full Retirement is reached	Unlimited	

In Betty's case, if she starts collecting Social Security benefits at age sixty-two and continues to work, she will lose part of her benefit. For example, if she receives $1,200 a month from Social Security and works part-time at her old employer, making $20,000 a year, she will be taxed one dollar for every two she earns above the $12,000 allowance—-which will be $8,000.

"That's almost stupid…to work, I mean," Pat said.

"Not stupid to work; stupid to start receiving Social Security early if you know you're going to keep working. And it doesn't take much income to trigger the penalty," I said. "So, for people like us who'll keep working at least until our mid-sixties, it doesn't make much sense to collect our money at sixty-two."

Benefits for a Spouse

Charlie poured more tea for himself and offered us the same. We both shook our heads. I'd had enough tea to float away. I didn't know where Charlie could possibly put all that liquid. He sipped the hot cup.

In the case of Charlie and Pat, here are some numbers to consider in making your decisions.

| Charlie's SS benefit | $3,000/month |
| Pat's SS benefit | $2,300/month |

When you retire, both of you would start receiving this amount. We'll also suppose that you both are at the full retirement age. For you that's sixty-six. If you die first, Charlie, Pat has the option of increasing her benefit to $3,000/month by switching to your level. If she dies first, you just keep getting your larger benefit. Nothing changes.

Pat leaned forward. "What happens if Charlie takes his at 62?"

"That's the point. Again, let's suppose your benefit at 62 is $2,100/month, Charlie. Notice that if you die first, Pat can choose to switch to your level, but…"

Considering that women usually outlive men for many years, she could potentially lose thousands of dollars. Seven hundred a month times 12 equals $8,400 a year. And if she lives for another ten years, that's $84,000 she would lose.

This is the big key that most people never think about when they're deciding when to start taking their benefits. Particularly for the men. For the women, it's different. If they start at sixty-two and the husband dies first, they get his benefit. So it might make sense for the wife to start at sixty-two and the husband start at sixty-six.

Pat nodded her head. "Nobody at work even knows about this. This makes a huge difference for women! The numbers Charlie used came out to $84,000 but what if I lived fifteen years longer? That would be over $100,000 in benefits lost."

Since 1986 people receiving Social Security benefits sometimes had to pay taxes on that income. How much were those taxes?

Taxes on Social Security Benefits

I started, "We've learned about the fact the government taxes your benefits and so do some states. Remember, this was part of the 'avalanche of taxes' we covered a few months ago?"

There are some strategies to minimize this or avoid it. That's why we talked about moving money out of IRA's and 401(K)'s into Roth IRA's…because you're not forced to take it out under the Required Minimum Distribution rules. But it's a big problem for lots of folks. The total taxable Social Security benefits in 1999 were $75.08 billion, which climbed to $93.5 billion in 2001. So, it's hitting many, many people.

"I thought the Congress had reduced taxes in the early 2000's under President Bush?" Pat said.

They did. On income taxes. They didn't touch Social Security taxes. Income tax rates are at an all-time low at 10% for some income. But Social Security taxes can go as high as marginal tax rates of 70%–90% (when you include state taxes) on some beneficiaries! Up to 85% of the benefit I receive may be subject to full tax.

If you're receiving SS benefits, here are strategies to reduce taxes.

1.   If you're working, try to defer income to future years, don't collect it now

2.   Don't take distributions from IRA's, pensions, 401(K)'s (Assuming you haven't reached 70 ½ and are forced to take it out)

3.   Shift assets to non-taxable resources like permanent life insurance

4.   Shift assets to resources that don't require the minimum distributions like Roth's or variable annuities

5.   Shift assets that produce income to other family members when you have enough to live on and don't need more income. This gets the asset and its income away from you.

Maximizing IRA's, 401(K)'s income

The third traditional source of income for retirement, are 401(K)'s, IRA's, deferred compensation, tax-sheltered annuities, and many others like these. Later, we'll learn about unusual, newer sources.

The starting point is to roll over everything to a self-directed IRA. (A self-directed IRA means that the investor gets to run it and make decisions about the plan, rather than a third party, working with the employer.)

Whether you're in regular IRA's or Roth IRAs, there comes a point when you have to figure out how to turn these assets into an income for you. People don't realize it, but ultimately **all** retirement assets are about creating a source of income for yourselves.

"Can't I just start taking money out as I need it?" Pat said.

What if you're taking too much and you run out? Or what if you could be taking more? Let's suppose you've got $100,000 in your Roth. You need about $6,500 a year to supplement your other sources, pensions and Social Security. You could start selling funds from your Roth at a rate of 6.5% a year. Of course it's not taxed so you get an advantage. From a regular IRA, you might get hit with a marginal tax rate of almost 30% with federal and state taxes, which means you'd only be left with $4,650 in your pockets after paying the taxes.

"That's exactly the lesson from the Roth conversion process we talked about. In a taxable account, to net $6,500 a year, you'd have to take out over 9% a year," Pat said.

"How do you know what percentage to take out?" Charlie asked. "Do you just figure out what you need per month?"

It's a question that's puzzled economists for years. There have been countless scholarly studies done over the years. The problem is the market. If the stock market's going up year after year, then even as you take money out of your Roth IRA, the growth you're experiencing "replaces" the money you're taking out of your Roth. But what happens when the market crashes? And stays down for several years? The average bear market lasts about one and a half years, but there have certainly been longer ones.

"I understand," said Pat. "As you're taking money out, the market's also 'taking money out' at the same time. It's a double whammy. And between the two, if you take out too much money, you could run out."

"So is there a percentage that we can use that will give us a pretty good chance of not running out?" Charlie said.

Start with two factors: the withdrawal rate and your Asset Allocation model. Here's a common error made by people who retire at younger ages. They worry about the ups and downs of the market so they move all their holdings into conservative, fixed-income or income funds, like bonds. Maybe they earn 5.5%.

I leaned forward with my green pen and found a clean napkin.

Fixed-income/bond portfolio grows at	5.5%
Less yearly withdrawals of	-4.5%
Less effects of inflation	-2.8%
Net effect on portfolio	-1.8%

"You can see that this retired person is going backwards. It's just a question of time before she runs out of money—even thought she 'thinks' she's being very careful and conservative."

"We're back to our Asset Allocation model and why it's important to not have all our eggs in one basket," Pat said.

There have been many studies conducted about this. For instance, in 1994, Roger Bengen in California started the discussion by publishing a paper that said a withdrawal rate of between 4.5% and 5% would have a 100% chance of **not** running out more than 30 years. Then, there's the Trinity University study from San Antonio that came up with the number of 4%. And the most recent was another study last fall by Jonathon Guyton that suggested withdrawal rates as high as 6.2%.

Bengen Study

William Bengen, "Determining Withdrawal Rates Using Historical Data",
Journal of Financial Planning, 10/1994
Portfolio comprised of at least 50% stock funds, preferably 75%

1.   Start with initial withdrawal rate of 4.5%–5%

2.   Increase each subsequent yearly withdrawal by the rate of inflation

3.   If you don't need as much as 5% a year, withdraw less

His study showed a 100% chance of your money lasting for 30 years. Remember Monte Carlo predictions, also. What is the probability that a person would not run out of money?

It's software that takes into account the performance of investments to be able to predict the chances that your money will last. It's very powerful stuff. Bengen said that if you started a withdrawal rate of 5% you had a 90% chance that your money would last for thirty years. At a starting rate of 5.25% the chances went down to 80%.

"But 80%–90% is still quite good, isn't it?" said Pam. "I think I'd take those odds. And these studies mean that you take your income out regardless of what the market is doing. I mean, if it's down, you still take your income?

Guyton Study

Jon Guyton, "Decision Rules and Portfolio Management for Retirees: Is the 'Safe" Initial Withdrawal Rate Too Safe?" Call for Papers submission to the <u>Journal of Financial Planning,</u> 2004

1. Portfolio has 80% stock funds and 20% income funds

2. Initial withdrawal rate is 6.2%

3. Generate cash and rebalance a diversified portfolio by selling winning funds

4. Cap annual withdrawal rates a 6% regardless of inflation

5. Withdrawals aren't increased after a year of negative investment returns

"I want to look at some actual numbers for us. That makes more sense to me," Pat said. "Suppose we have $650,000 in our Roths. Let's see…" She took my pen from me and scratched over the paper.

$650,000   4.8% = $31,200/year or $2,600/month income

$650,000   6.2% = $40,300/year or $3,358/month income

She chewed on her knuckle. "We'd have $758 a month more with the higher withdrawal rate. That makes a huge difference! Seems pretty obvious to me, Charlie. We should consider using about 6% of our money for living on."

There are a couple things to keep in mind. **All the studies** I've seen show that even after you retire, you must keep your portfolio aggressive. You can dial it back a little, but the long-term results show that the aggressive portfolios—those more heavily tilted towards holding lots of stock funds rather than bond funds—-always outperformed the alternatives as an income-producing vehicle. The years when this kind of a portfolio underperformed, the difference was relatively small.

"Gimme that in English."

"An aggressive portfolio will give you all the advantages with few of the disadvantages."

Most people don't follow any of these well thought-out studies. They've never learned the lessons of these studies and mistakenly think that the minute they retire, they should turn very conservative. At 80, it's a different story but at 60 or even 70, most people have a long life still ahead of them and need to make their money last.

"So you're saying that most people fear that the market will go down and they'll see their monthly statements with 'losses' but the real thing they should fear is that they'll run out of money!" Pat said.

Another interesting idea that's popped up is from the Behavioral Economists. These are researchers that study not only the economy but also how people **really** act in life, not in a perfect economic model. Those studies seem to show that people tend to spend more in the early years of retirement and less as they get older.

"Makes sense. People start to slowdown as they get older." Charlie said.

"With this in mind, maybe it's okay to spend more than 6% for the first years of your retirement…I'm not sure."

"To me, it makes sense to keep checking every few years, like we've done over the years with you," said Pat. "Keep planning and fine-tuning as we go."

"What I'm interested in, is what happens to those people who don't have pensions, 401(K)'s or haven't saved enough to retire but they still want to?"

Newer Sources of Income

"I've read the savings rate in America is down to zero," Pat said. "Does that mean there are lots of people who won't be able to afford to retire when they want?"

That seems to be the way things are pointing. Especially with the baby boomers. We've learned they don't have a lot of the advantages their parents had at retirement time. But there are some new, unusual ways to create retirement income. Some of these are going to sound heretical to some people but if they work, why not use them.

Immediate Annuities

"What are those? I've never heard about this," Charlie said.

Annuities are contracts with an insurance company where you invest money into the contract. They can be set-up to grow at fixed rates, like a CD or you can invest in a group of mutual funds, more like an IRA. Your money grows tax-deferred and when you take money out, you only pay tax on the growth portion, not the money you originally put in. They are like super I.O.U.'s, in that the insurance company guarantees to pay you back, in some form, in the future. These become very secure, dependable sources of income for the owners.

"Those are called fixed or variable annuities, aren't they?" Pat said.

There is a third kind also. An Immediate Annuity is one where you put money into a contract with an insurance company and they begin immediately to pay you a monthly income that **you can never outlive.**

"Wait a minute! Isn't that the problem we just talked about? We didn't want to outlive our money and now you're saying there's a way to do it?" Charlie said.

Think of it like a "backward mortgage". With a mortgage, you borrow cash from a bank to buy your house. Depending on the amount you've borrowed, how many years you have to pay it back, and the interest rate, that will determine your monthly payment.

"Yeah…like the shorter the time, fifteen years, let's say, the bigger the monthly payment."

An Immediate Annuity is just backwards. You give a lump of money to an insurance company. Depending on how many years they think you're going to live and the prevailing interest rates, they guarantee to pay you a monthly amount for as long as you live. The monthly income will be higher or lower depending on your life expectancy, and the interest rate. It's a way for a person to create their own pension, that's guaranteed to provide income for as long as they live.

Pat said, "Sounds good. Why don't we just take our entire Roth IRA and invest in an immediate annuity?"

"'Cause of one problem: inflation. The payment you get is fixed for the rest of your life and won't go up to cover inflation. Or, if you die earlier than expected, the deal is the insurance company keeps all your money and the monthly payments end."

They work best if the retired person doesn't have a pension. Many people are fearful to set-up their portfolios at retirement in an aggressive manner. To help with this, they could invest in an immediate annuity. Again, there are scholarly studies that show we shouldn't use more than 25%–50% of your assets to buy an annuity. Too much money spent on an annuity leaves you without inflation protection. On the other hand, you need to invest enough to create a large enough monthly income to help yourself.

I told them about two clients of mine to illustrate the use of immediate annuities.

Fred and Wilma are two people in their late 70's. Both worked at jobs that didn't pay a lot but both saved into their 401(K)'s so they have about $500,000 in their Roth's—they converted at my urging—but don't have any pension income. They're collecting Social Security but that's not enough for them since they help their children and grandchildren financially as they can. Fred was an electrician and Wilma worked at a bank as a teller for many years until she was promoted into the personal loan department. Unfortunately, it was a small bank and they didn't have a pension program but they did have a 401(K) to which Wilma contributed what she could.

They're in good health but are very cautious about their money. Each time I tried to reassure them with all the academic studies that showed better results with aggressive portfolios, they became green…about the color of cabbage. I try to tell them that with a more aggressive portfolio, they could probably raise their rate of withdrawal. Of course, at the same time, I never push my clients beyond their comfort level. If they can't sleep at night, what's the point?

They need more income but are too conservative to change.

That's where an immediate annuity can be helpful in combination with money invested in the market. See, it's the uncertainty that bothers Fred and Wilma and they'd like to have some guarantees about this. The stock market doesn't guarantee anything. One way to handle this is to invest in an immediate annuity which converts some of their retirement assets into a stream of income that is guaranteed for as long as they live.

"I can certainly understand their comfort level would be higher with the addition of an annuity," Pat said. "Of course, that means they'll have less money to grow for themselves."

The trade off in comfort level is worth it to them. And the studies show that the addition of an annuity decreases what's called the "longevity risk", that is, they may outlive their money supply. From a Monte Carlo perspective, the probability of them running out of money decreases greatly.

Charlie said, "And they still have the majority of their retirement money in the market to keep up with inflation,"

"Yeah. Funny thing is, when we put this in place for Fred and Wilma, their willingness to take a little more risk with the money in the market rose. 'Cause they knew they had their own 'pension' that would always be there for them."

Reverse Mortgages

"Our bank is running lots of ads for reverse mortgages," Pat said, "it doesn't sound right to me. Should we look at them? They're awfully new, aren't they?"

I shrugged. "They seem new 'cause all the banks suddenly started advertising them. Actually, they've been around for a long time. But with the historically low interest rates we've experienced lately, these products have become popular and they can be a huge benefit to people who haven't saved enough for retirement."

"It's been great for the consumer," Pat said and turned to me. "That explains why the banks are pushing reverse mortgages."

"They make a <u>lot</u> of money on them. That doesn't necessarily mean they're a bad product. Like most financial tools, they're good for certain circumstances. I call them 'last chance' opportunities."

They are "last chance" because they're very expensive and should only be used as a last resort. In fact, the expenses are the biggest drawback. Still, they're popular. In 2004, reverse mortgages reached record highs.

Here's the typical scenario where they work the best.

Fred and Wilma are 77 and 75. (You have to be at least 62 to qualify for a reverse Mortgage) They both receive Social Security benefits although they aren't much since neither had high-paying careers. Fred's got a small private pension that he's received since he retired at 62. Since it's not indexed for inflation, the purchasing power isn't much anymore. They've been able to manage over the years only because their house was paid off and they didn't have a mortgage payment. Their budget is squeezed because of medical costs that have increased significantly. They need more monthly income. Their health and ages are such that work isn't a possibility. How can they increase their income?

They could sell their home, of course, and use the equity to create some income but they don't want to move and even if they sold, they'd still need to pay rent somewhere else.

"So, a reverse mortgage comes in handy?"

It's a loan from a lender that provides a monthly income until the owner sells, dies, or moves out for more than 12 months. If any of those happen, the borrower (or their beneficiaries) must sell the house and pay back whatever's owing. They will never owe more that the value of the home, even if the home drops in value. Like a regular mortgage, the lender figures an interest rate, the value of the home, and how long they think the borrower will live in order to determine the monthly payment.

The owner keeps title to the home, by the way and the lender can't force the borrower out of their home, even if the value of the home drops. Another nice feature is that payments are tax-free to the borrower since it's a loan. The lender will look at about 65%–70% of the value of the house to set the monthly payment.

"Not the full value?" Charlie said. "Well, I suppose they need a cushion in case the borrower lives to be 110 years old!"

In addition, this income doesn't count toward Social Security or Medicare benefits; it won't reduce these. Because a person is technically "borrowing" this, it's not counted as income. There are no income or credit requirements to qualify.

"It actually sounds very attractive," said Pat. "Why don't you like them?"

"I didn't say I don't like them," I corrected her. "When the borrower dies, for instance, the heirs have to sell the house, pay back the amount borrowed up to that point, and pay the fees—that's where the lender's clean up. The fees can be very high."

Here are some other tips.

1.   The older the person, the higher the payments because they won't live as long.

2.   Try to delay applying for one as long as possible

3.   The location of the property is crucial. Obviously, more desirable areas will be appraised higher but in addition, the lender will feel confident that the property will sell easier and quicker

4.   You should shop around to find the lowest fees and the best appraisal

5.   Reverse mortgages may also apply to condos, townhouses, and manufactured homes on an owned lot. (Second homes, lake places, condos in Florida, and any property that's not the borrower's main residence aren't eligible)

"Sounds like these work best for elderly people who are in cash-flow trouble," Pat said.

"Sure but in the coming lesson, we'll talk about those people who want to retire but find they haven't saved enough money," I said. I unwrapped my fortune cookie and laid it on the table. I retrieved the small paper. Lifted it. "You will come into a lot of money," it said.

What my notes said

1. I taught Pat and Charlie where to find sources of income for retirement. They should learn this before they retired, which would help them make the decision when to retire.

2. We looked at maximizing pension income and strategies to increase this with the use of life insurance.

3. We looked at maximizing Social Security benefits and were able to answer the question of what age should they start taking their benefits?

4. We learned how to maximize the income potential of 401(K)'s, IRA's, deferred compensation, and tax-sheltered annuities.

5. I showed them some excellent studies done to answer the question of how much income could they take from their retirement funds without running out of money before they died.

6. I introduced Immediate Annuities as a resource to create a "private pension" that a person could never outlive, as a source of income in retirement.

7. I educated them about reverse mortgages and, for people who have not saved enough of retirement to create adequate income to live on, these products can help.

Lesson Five:
Learn to create new sources of income for yourself

Lesson Five:
Learn to create new sources of income for yourself

Chapter Eleven

What's the smart thing to do with inherited money?

"Although you're not 'creating' a new source of income immediately, if you're fortunate enough to inherit some assets, there are good ways to turn this into a source of income for you," I started.

"I think this might happen to us," Pat said, "although I'm certainly not waiting for it or depending on it. I've read there's almost 3 trillion dollars in assets that Baby Boomers stand to receive."

Charlie said, "And if we happen to get anything from our parents, what should we do with it?"

There are three things for you to consider initially.

——Save some of it!!

——Keep as much away from the IRS as possible

——Use a strategy to convert an asset to a stream of income.

"I've seen studies of people who've won the lottery. I can't remember what percentage of them have nothing left after five years," Pat said. "I think it's as high as 60–70% of those people spend everything!"

In some ways, it's not their fault. All of us are human and most of us aren't used to dealing with huge chunks of money. Maybe I'd do the same thing…I don't know. But if I have a chance, I try to help my clients preserve as much as possible. In fact, the first piece of advice I give them is to not do anything for a few months. For some of my clients, I tell them to sit on it for six months. Let the idea sink in. Try not to change your day to day life at all for awhile.

Pat said, "That makes a lot of sense. But you have to make decisions at some point."

The first question: how much should I save? What percentage? And that depends on your other assets and your situation. For instance, if you haven't saved much for your own retirement and you're 58 years old, by all means, put 90+% into some kind of retirement plan to create a stream of income later. On the other hand, if you've fully funded your retirement plans and you have several sources of income for your retirement, then you could start to think of what your children may inherit or a group, like a church, could get.

"What could we do?" Pat leaned forward.

1. Depending on how much you inherit, you still may be wondering if you have enough to live on the rest of your lives. That means you should follow all the lessons we learned before. For instance, use the **Monte Carlo modeling** to see what probability there is that your money will last.

2. Open a **Roth IRA** for each spouse and fully fund it for several years

3. Start a variable or fixed-rate **Annuity** and put whatever you have left over after funding the Roths into it. Unlike a Roth, the annuity doesn't have a maximum amount you are limited to invest per year. And the growth is tax-deferred.

4. If you have a **Permanent Life Insurance** policy or are young enough and need one, this is a good alternative. Like an annuity, you're not limited in the amount you can invest each year, the growth is tax-deferred, and you can borrow from yourself, tax free.

5. You could invest in a family of **Mutual Funds**, using your Asset Allocation model to pick the funds. This alternative would enable you to have immediate access to the funds, unlike the annuity or life insurance policy

6. You could use a **Combination** of Roths, annuities, life insurance, and a family of mutual funds, depending on your situation

7. You should use your **Asset Allocation Model** for all these investments
8. You could also **Add to your present Retirement Plans** such as a 401(K). You learned before why this is probably the last thing you should do to avoid the future tax problems. But as with any of these lessons, they work for different people in different situations.

Here's an example of two clients I worked with last month.

Jack and Jill worked for private corporations and had 401(K) retirement plans. Here's what they could contribute:

Jacks' salary	$90,000
Contribution limits	5%
Amount Jack could Contribute	$4,500/yr.
Jill's salary	$110,000
Contribution limits	6%
Amount Jill could contribute	$6,600/yr

When they came to me, they hadn't contributed anything to either plan for the present year.

Then, Jill inherited $150,000 from her mother. They wanted to spend $50,000 fixing up the house and improving it. I said—okay—but be sure to save the rest! At their income level, they were getting killed by taxes. Both were in the top federal and state income tax brackets.

I had them take about one-third, $33,300, and put it into a Money Market fund. Then, during the first year, both of them had the maximum contribution to each of their 401(K) plans deducted from their paychecks and put into their401(K)s. To make-up for the smaller checks, they drew exactly $11,100 a year, or almost $1,000 a month, from their Money Market account.

Since their paychecks were smaller by $11,100 that year, their taxes went down by about $4,000, state and federal. So, they saved the inherited money and were also able to save on taxes. In year two, they deducted the maximum deductions from their paychecks and lived on the second $11,100 in the Money Market account. And, of course, the third year, they did the same.

"Why did you only go for three years?" Pat asked.

They had to tie-up a lot of money in the low-yielding Money Market funds as it was. I didn't want them to put in everything. There were more productive places to invest, as you've learned.

Pat said, "Did either of their employers match their contributions?"

I said, "Yeah, each employer matched up to 3% of their salary. So let's see… that added about $6,000 a year to each 401(K)."

Pat smiled. "You're positively crooked!" She joked. "So let's see myself…what you got them to do."

$11,100/yr	into the 401(K)s
$4,000/yr	in saved income taxes
<u>$6,000/yr</u>	in employer's matching contributions
$21,100/yr.	Total "savings"

"And then, you multiplied that by three years! You took $33,300 of their inherited money to start with and 'created' an extra $30,000 for them! That's got to be illegal!"

"It's just a smart way to make good use of inherited money. Normally, I don't recommend maxing-out the 401(K) but you can see that in their case, it made great sense."

"What about Uncle Sam? You said to avoid taxes. Is this example what you meant?" Charlie said.

There are many ways that you may get an inheritance. Typically, there are five ways to receive this kind of money.

1. Receive cash—usually from a life insurance policy of which you were the beneficiary.
2. You could get personal property—cars, jewelry, furniture, etc.
3. You could inherit real estate—most often the homestead
4. Stocks, bonds, mutual funds, etc.
5. You could be the beneficiary of your parent's IRAs

Because of changes in the tax laws and the way these first four items are valued, you may not have to pay any inheritance or income taxes on any of these. Obviously, you can convert any of these first four things to cash and invest it. Or leave the present investments where they are. Later, after retirement, you can use the strategies we've learned to create new sources of income for yourself.

"You've left out IRAs. Is that a big deal? I mean, how many of these will our generation get?" Pat asked.

"Plenty! A lot of that 3 trillion you talked about is locked up in IRAs—which is okay because you'll see in a minute, why this is a wonderful way to inherit money. And, therefore, is another reason why both of you should have IRAs and Roth IRAs."

"What do you mean, Charlie?" Pat said. "You said 'wonderful'."

"Well, if handled correctly, they can be used to preserve and increase inherited money for <u>many</u> years. They're called **Stretch IRA's**, because you can 'stretch' them over many years."

Here's an example of some clients I worked with last year.

Marge died at age 86. She'd established an IRA years earlier, naming her two sons, Bill and Bob, as beneficiaries of the IRA. By doing so, the minute she died, ownership automatically transferred to the boys.

Bill was 56 and Bob 54 at the time of their mother's death. The value of the IRA was $500,000, so each boy inherited a "Beneficiary IRA" (A special kind the IRS has established for these situations) of $250,000 each. Since Marge was over 70 ½, she'd been taking her Required Minimum Distribution for years, but always took the minimum out. In the meantime, her IRA had continued to grow quite nicely. Now, the boys each inherited half.

"Since the boys are under 70 ½, I suppose the RMD drops off for them and they can let the money grow tax deferred," Pat said.

Because Marge had started her RMD, the boys had to continue—but at their own rate based on each one's age at the time of her death. Here's a chart from the IRS to use in calculating the amount they must take out.

Single Life Expectancy Table for Inherited IRAs

35	48.5
36	47.5
37	46.5
38	45.6
39	44.6
40	43.6
41	42.7
42	41.7
43	40.7
44	39.8
45	38.8
46	37.9
47	37.0
48	36.0
49	35.1
50	34.2
51	33.3
52	32.3
53	31.4
54	30.5
55	29.6
56	28.7
57	27.9
58	27.0
59	26.1
60	25.2
61	24.4
62	23.5
63	22.7
64	21.8
65	21.0
66	20.2
67	19.4
68	18.6
69	17.8
70	17.0
71	16.3
72	15.5
73	14.8
74	14.1
75	13.4

"So how does this work?" Pat said. "How do you figure this out?"

Let's go back to our example.

First, we look at Bill, who was age 56 when his mother died. The calculation is easy. We follow down the chart to age 56 and read across to the factor, 28.7.

The green pen came out and I wrote.

$250,000 divided by 28.7 = $8,710

Therefore, Bill must take out $8,710 the first year. The second year, he'd take the same value but decrease the factor by 1.0%.

"But where does the term 'stretch' fit in?"

"Simple. Try dividing $8,710 by the original value of $250,000 to see what percentage you're really taking out of the IRA."

The percentage was 3.4%.

Charlie said, "Do you think Bill can get the Beneficiary IRA to grow better than 3.4% a year?"

"Sure. And even after he takes out the required minimum, it's still growing so it'll stretch out for years after the mom died."

It's a great advantage to Bill. Suppose Marge created the IRA when she was 31 years old. That means she received tax-deferred growth for 55 years until her death. Now Bill starts it at his age of 56. Suppose he lives until 82. Now, this original investment has been 'stretched' over a total of 81 tax deferred years! (It can't go any longer than Bill's life) Of course, if he wants to create a bigger stream of income than $8,710 a year, he can always take more out of the Beneficiary IRA. It may not last as long but he's got the income he needs. And once the right combination of investments is chosen, Bill will have the opportunity for several sources of income.

"So, all the lessons you've been teaching us could be applied to inherited money," Pat said. "It just gives the person a 'jump start' by inheriting the extra money."

"It's a wonderful blessing if you get something like this. But what if you don't? What are other ways to create sources of income?" I said.

Can we find any <u>more</u> ways to get more income for ourselves?

A couple weeks later, our next financial lesson appointment arrived. I drove to my office. As I walked from the car, the early summer humidity hit me. Circled in warm, heavy air, it felt clammy. Luckily, I'd worn casual clothes to work and didn't mind the heat.

How's everyone?" I asked them when they were seated next to me. "We're going to continue in our lessons about finding new ways to create sources of income for your retirement today. Let's see…where did we leave off?"

More income using Annuities

We'll start with the use of annuities again. There are very creative ways to use them that most people don't know anything about. So often in financial decisions, success is just a matter of re-positioning your assets. Today, we're trying to create more income.

Pat said, "You've said that one of the big advantages of annuities is their flexibility,"

You pay extra for some of the advantages but if you shop around, you can find many annuities with reasonable fees. I'll tell you a story of a client I recently helped.

Helmer, a retired college professor, had been widowed. He continued to teach until he was 65, quit, and started collecting his state pension and Social Security. He and his wife loved to travel so after she died and he received a $100,000 death benefit, he put it all in a CD.

His plan was to take an extraordinary trip, in honor of his wife, and draw an income from the interest on the CD to help pay expenses. He decided to get a Harley and start tracing the "blue highways" out to San Diego, where the couple had been married years before.

Typical of a college professor, Helmer studied the cycle, how it worked, and how to ride it. He even took lessons on riding. As he prepared for the expedition, he realized that he wouldn't have enough income to pay all his expenses. He didn't want to raid his IRA but the CD paid 7% (this was a few years ago!) which, of course, created an income of $7,000 a year. Or, after taxes (Marginal fed and state rates about 30%) it left him with $4,900. That's $408 a month.

This wasn't quite enough. When he came to me, Helmer told me his friends said the only thing to do was start taking principal and interest from the CD. The income alone, wouldn't be enough.

He was a conservative fellow and really wanted to preserve his capital. As a college professor, he hadn't earned much and what he had left was all he would ever have. I could understand perfectly.

He asked me, "Is there a way to increase my income and, at the same time, preserve the principal?"

Of course, there's a way. Here are the numbers. Remember, this strategy will work for anyone. That's what I want you to learn. Start with his CD. We're going cash it in and invest in two annuities. We call it "split funding."

Original Amount

$100,000

Split in the following manner

Amount to an Immediate Annuity For tax-favored income	Amount to a deferred fixed-rate Annuity to grow tax-deferred
$29,750	Interest rate= 7.35%
Guaranteed monthly income $583	$70,250
Guaranteed annual income $7,000 (85% tax free)	
Total payout in 5 years $35,000	5 years of tax-deferred compounding grows to total= $100,151

"The immediate annuity cost him $29,750 to buy it?" Pat said.

"Yeah. From the $100,000 CD, we used that amount to create an income for him that was larger, after tax, than his $408 by almost $200 a month."

"What's this 85% tax-free thing?" Charlie asked.

"You only pay tax on the <u>growth</u> portion of an annuity when you take money out. You never pay tax on the part coming out that represents your investment. The usual formula is about 85% is tax-free."

"And then, in five years, the second annuity has grown back to the original amount of the CD."

"Yes. There are lots of ways to fool around with this idea but my example gives you the guts of the strategy. There are all kinds of ways to use different tools to create more income."

Use your home to create a source of income

Twenty million Americans over 62 have homes that are paid off. They own them free and clear. It's been estimated that this represents $2 trillion of equity. Yet, here's the irony: many of these same people say their budgets are pinched and they're worried it'll get worse. As the enemy, inflation, eats away at their purchasing power, they feel the effects and have a hard time making ends meet.

"They're looking for extra income." Charlie said.

"I'm not talking about people who have very little, if any, assets, those who's only source of income is Social Security. What I'm going to teach you doesn't apply to these people."

"So, we're looking at couples who may've already done some of the things you've gone over but still need to supplement their income," Charlie said.

1. Many Americans, even those who haven't paid-off their mortgages, still have lots of equity in their homes

2. Equity doesn't "earn" money; it doesn't have a rate of return

Charlie interrupted me, "Our home's gone up in value by almost 7% a year in the last three years. I know that may not continue but doesn't this prove our equity's grown? Therefore, how can you say it doesn't have a rate of return? Seems to me, it's about 7% a year."

Good question. And you're not alone—everyone asks me the same question. But you're confusing two different things. Your house is an asset, of course, but it's your <u>house</u> that's grown at 7%. Equity growth depends on both the increase in the value of the house and the amount you pay-down your mortgage each year."

"I think I get it," said Pat, "whether we have 100% equity in our house—it's paid off—or none, the <u>house</u> still increases in value. Equity has nothing to do with the rate of increase in the value."

Remember the lesson about not paying off your mortgage. This ties-in. The point is that the amount of equity in your home is separate from the increase in the value of your home. The two things aren't connected.

"Okay," Charlie said although I could tell that the concept still didn't sit easily with him.

Everyone I know always talked about the increase in their equity. They were correct, equity grew, but in and of itself, it had no rate of return.

1. | House value | = | $300,000 |
   |---|---|---|
   | Equity in house | = | $100,000 |
   | Increase is market | | |
   | Value | = | 7% |
   | New house value | = | $321,000 |
   | (1 year later) | | |
   | New home equity | = | $121,000 |
   | Net increase in equity | = | +$21,000 |

2. | House value | = | $300,000 |
   |---|---|---|
   | Equity in house | = | 0 |
   | Increase in market | | |
   | Value | = | 7% |
   | New House value | = | $321,000 |
   | (1 year later) | | |
   | New Home equity | = | $21,000 |
   | Net increase in equity | = | +$21,000 |

The amount of equity in a house had nothing to do with the growth of the equity. Either way, there still was the same net increase in equity. Most people don't understand the separation between rate of return and equity. Once you do understand, we can move on.

"You're gonna separate the equity in a house from the house itself, I bet," Pat said.

Charlie stopped us. "Wait a minute. The people I know, view the equity in their homes as almost 'holy' money. They don't want to tamper with it. They include it in their net worth. You've told me that almost every client of your's lists their home as the best investment they've ever made."

Today, equity's no longer 'holy' money. Have you seen the figures for home equity or line of credit loans? They've skyrocketed to all-time high levels. And a lot of that money coming out's going to consumer goods—cars, boats, golf clubs, and vacations unfortunately.

This is about something a little different. Once we get in our minds that the equity in your house not only doesn't have to stay with the house but that it actually isn't "doing anything" inside your house, you can begin to see ways to get it out and get it working to create some income.

Should a person take all the equity out? Is that prudent? Most people feel a lot better with some equity in their house. What if the price drops? What if they sell and need to pay for real estate agent's commissions, and things like that? They need the "cushion" of equity in their homes for very practical reasons.

Some of the studies recommend taking <u>all</u> of your equity out of your home. You can do it with these new interest-only mortgages and design it so that you really pay nothing down when you buy a new home.

"I feel the same way you do," I said. "I'm from the 'old school' where we were just a little bit more conservative. Personally, I'm more comfortable with about 15%–20% equity in a home. Like you said, it gives a little cushion to the owners in case there's trouble."

"If you leave only 20% equity in the house, what do you recommend doing with the money that's come out?" Pat said.

Here's a model. Not all financial advisors like this idea but it can work as a resource for extra income for some people. Particularly, those who have not saved enough to live on after they quit working.

1. Equity left from sale of first house $250,000

     Purchase price of new home $500,000

     Down payment (50%) $250,000

     Mortgage amount $250,000

     Mortgage payment (30 yr @ 6%) $1,498

In the mortgage payment, we're ignoring taxes and insurance to make a point. What's the real cost of the mortgage payment after taxes? Assuming this couple is in about the 30% marginal rate with federal and state.

The calculator figured that the net cost of the payment was: $1,049.

I wrote $1,049 below the figure for the mortgage payment. Because the government allows you to deduct the interest on a mortgage payment, it "reduces" your payment by the amount of saved income taxes…in this case, down to $1,049 or $12,590 a year. Now let's look at taking some of the equity out of the new home.

2. Equity from sale of first home $250,000
    Purchase price of new home $500,000
    Down payment (20%) $100,000
    Mortgage amount $400,000
    Mortgage payment (30 yr @ 6%) $2,398
    After-tax cost of payment $1,678

We get a difference of $629 a month or $7,557 a year more when we put only 20% equity into the new home. Let's follow the appreciation of this house for a year.

3. Value of new home $500,000 @ 7% = $535,000
    Growth of equity   +$35,000   = $285,000
    Value of new home $500,000 @ 7% = $535,000
    Growth of equity   +$35,000   = $135,000

Growth in the equity's the same, obviously, at $35,000. But with example number one, you've got $285,000 in equity in the house.

In example number two, you wouldn't leave the extra $150,000 in loose equity lying around! You'd do something with it.

"Well…you could buy a CD," Charlie said.

"Not a great return," Pat said, "how about a bond fund? One that returned, oh say, 6.0% a year."

Add that into the calculations.

4.	Growth in equity in new house	+$35,000
	Growth of the bond funds	
	($150,000 @ 6.0%)	+$ 9,000
	Total for both	+$44,000

This looks much better.

"Wait a minute. You're forgetting that you're paying more for the second mortgage. You gotta figure that in by subtracting it from the gain in the bond funds," Pat said.

"Okay, perfectly good idea. How much extra, after tax, was that?"

I looked back over my notes. "$7,557."

5.	Growth in equity in new house	+$35,000
	Growth for bonds funds	+$ 9,000
	Less extra cost of mortgage payments	-$ 7,557
	Total for both	+$36,543

This is where we end up. In the first example when we put down 50% equity we had an increase of $35,000 at the end of the first year. By only putting down 20% and investing the difference, we ended up with a total of $36,543. This is just for one year. Remember if you keep doing this for several years, the power of compounding will really push example number two, off the charts. And there's something else beneficial–liquidity. You've freed up that equity to work for you and you can get at it, if you needed it. You could always sell some of the bond funds for extra cash.

Let's go yet another step further with another strategy. Why not use the extra income from the bond fund to help pay for the higher mortgage? After all, one of the reasons people give me for paying-off the mortgage, is that during retirement, they don't want the financial obligation to make payments. Over the years, if they had taken equity out of their homes and invested it, it's possible the outside investments could produce enough income to pay a big chunk of the mortgage payment for them, without touching the principal that's invested.

"Great idea. What's the downside?"

"I have a few 'rules' I think people should follow before using this strategy."

a.   Always try to borrow at a lower interest rate than you can earn with the equity you invest. Lately, this has been possible with the low mortgage rates.

b.   Be very careful with adjustable rate, no interest, and other types of artificially low interest loans. When the larger payments come due, the advantage of borrowing at low rates and investing at higher rates may be lost

c.   Clearly, you can deduct the interest payments you make on the mortgage but it's best if you can invest in something outside that grows tax-deferred and has tax-free or at least reduced taxes when you take out income. A good vehicle for this is permanent life insurance that we learned about before. Money inside the policy grows tax-deferred and may be "borrowed" by way of an income, tax-free. The combination of deductibility of mortgage interest to reduce taxes and the tax-deferred, tax-free use of the invested money is very powerful

d.   I think the outside investments should be extremely conservative. The idea here is to try and conserve your equity so that it continues to have a good chance to grow in the coming years. Speculative investments may wipe-out your equity and you're left with very little income sources and a big mortgage.

What my notes said

1.   If people were fortunate enough to inherit money, there were smart ways to invest it to create additional sources of income. The use of Roth IRA's, annuities, permanent life insurance, and a family of mutual funds were all good vehicles to use.

2.   I showed them they could increase their income with the creative use of annuities. Particularly, by "splitting" an existing annuity into two types: an immediate annuity and a fixed annuity. This would work to create a source of income, while preserving some of the cash.

3.   I taught them that they could separate some, or all, of the equity from their home and invest it in a conservative manner. This could create another source of income while giving the person greater liquidity.

Chapter Twelve

Start your own corporation for more income

It's obvious that if you start a small business you can create more income, but people don't realize how much better this is than going to work for someone else. There are a variety of advantages and it's the exact opposite from being an employee.

When you're an employee, every expense, like pensions, health care, and taxes are deducted first, then you get your check. You pay taxes on the gross amount you earn. I'm always listening to people who complain about how little they actually get in their paycheck after deductions. When you're in business for yourself or you incorporate, which is even better, you can deduct all the same things an employee does but your taxes are calculated on what's left over afterward. And it gets better since many of the things that you can legally deduct are both personal and business in nature. For instance, you can deduct a portion of the expense of your car that is used for Business. It helps reduce the cost of a car.

The power of a personal corporation is unknown to most people. Employees earn their pay and get taxed and get by with what remains in their paychecks. A personal corporation spends everything it can, is taxed on anything left over, and keeps a larger chunk of it's earnings in it's pockets.

"Isn't it complicated to form a corporation? Don't you need lots of people?" Pat asked me.

No. If you have a hobby business with a friend, you could start a corporation. You have a few legal papers to prepare and a small fee to pay to the state for recognizing you, but that's about it. Of course, the IRS says you must "act like a corporation" so you need to have a board of directors, meetings, keep notes and records, and other practices of a company. They're usually worth the time and effort. You also must have a true business purpose, other than avoiding taxes. So, a hobby business must be one that is a legitimate one that you are working at for more than fun. You must be working to make sales and grow your business.

"You think if a person has a small business, even one out of their home, that they should set up a corporation?" Pat said.

It's worth the time to take a careful look at the advantages. Another benefit is that you can take some of your gross income, set-up a retirement plan in the corporation for yourself, and deduct your contributions to the retirement plan on a pretax basis.   This retirement plan could be in addition to one your employer provides, if you're still working for someone else while starting your own business.

Look for a business that you like; something that you're familiar with. Especially since this is going be a retirement job, do something you've always wanted to do. Ideally, it won't have many start-up costs.

"When people come to me for advice on starting their own business, I find that one of the greatest problems is their lack of belief in themselves and the idea they have. Most people have worked as employees all their lives, so going out on their own is very scary," I said.

Pat said, "But do they do it eventually?"

"Some do. The funny thing is, when they do and have some success, even a little, you'd be amazed at how happy and thrilled they are!"

"It goes back to what we talked about weeks ago. That it's a good idea in retirement to challenge yourself. To do things that are a little uncomfortable, to stretch yourself. You're right, when these businesses work well, it's very satisfying."

Start small. Start the business in your basement, if you can. Keep your costs down as low as possible. As sales pick up, you can always add overhead. Many people, particularly men, who've been laid-off in mid-life, look for a new job for months and finally, decide they'd like to start their own business. They take all the money out of their 401(K) to invest in a "hot" new business idea. That's not a good idea. Your retirement money is sacred. It shouldn't be touched for something like this. Start small. There's the famous story of Steven Jobs starting Apple Computer in a garage. He didn't drop a half million dollars on the new business but built it as sales grew.

Depending on the business a person gets into, there are lots of ways to get other people to 'lend' you the money. For instance, if it's a retail business, suppliers are usually willing to send you product without collecting for 60–90 days. Hopefully, in the meantime, you sell it and can easily pay off the creditors.

"Why don't more people do this, if it's such a good deal?" Pat asked.

"I think it's because people don't know how simple a corporate form can be. They don't realize it can be a husband and wife, for instance. Sure, they should use a lawyer to help them set it up and an accountant would be good too, to help keep the financial records in correct form. But that's not too hard and not too expensive, either," I said.

For a lot of people thinking of quitting, the idea of part time work may be necessary. For others, it just adds a little to their retirement income and "gives them something to do." Either way, one should decide if you want to be an employee or you want to run your own business. Because of all the tax advantages to a corporation, it's possible a person could gross much less in their business, than working as an employee, but still end up with more cash.

Rental Opportunities for Income

"Here's another idea that people overlook. There could be rental opportunities all around them to take advantage of," I said.

Many middle class people own a home with at least a two-car garage and maybe they also have a lake cabin or a condo somewhere. Why not look for opportunities to rent space or vacation time with those assets?

"Oh sure," Pat said. "My parents used to rent out their lake home for a few weeks during the summer. Even after the extra costs for clean up and to pay for insurance, they made enough to pay all of their property taxes. And lake-shore property was taxed heavily."

"Perfect examples. Did they give-up their whole summer?"

"No. I think it was maybe, four to six weeks. But that was easy since they weren't at their cabin every single week anyway."

"Or maybe they could've rented some of their land during the winter to store a boat or two," I said.

"If they had a garage at the lake place, perhaps it had room to rent for someone else's car storage." I leaned over the table. "See. There's lots of these little opportunities. Maybe at your own home, you've got extra places that could be rented for some purpose. I know we're not talking about thousands of dollars with this idea, but a few hundred here and there can really help out."

"There could be a little hassle with renters and access but I could see where it might be worth it for the extra income," Charlie said. He paused, then said, "This doesn't apply to us, but what about those couples who want to retire but just haven't saved quite enough? What do you tell them to help find more income?"

Last Chance Ways to Create Income

"Actually, there are lots of people who come to me who haven't saved much but they still want to retire. My first, honest response is to caution them not to. To wait and try to sock away some more money. But I usually get the same response. They just want to quit." I sighed. "They usually have the same reasons, too."

"Which is?"

"'I've worked all my life. I deserve to retire. My parents retired at this age. All my friends are retired…You can imagine. So then, I have to move to Plan B which is the 'last chance' for these kinds of people. Of course, I don't tell 'em that."

The American savings rate is down to zero percent. If it wasn't for forced retirement plans with employers, I'm afraid of what we, as a country, would face with people wanting to retire in the next ten years. There are all kinds of statistics that show most people are not financially prepared to retire…but they will want to. It'll be hard for these people. They're unprepared and they don't know the pitfalls awaiting them, like inflation, taxes, loss of purchasing power. Add to this, the fact they haven't saved enough and you can see the perilous trip ahead of them.

They can start by taking advantage of some of the tools looked at already. Some of these ideas could help. The downside of this strategy is that they probably won't have much, if anything, left for their kids. So if they want to leave a chunk of money for their kids, this won't work.. However, lots of people aren't worried about that. They think it's their money and the kids can make it on their own.

"What would you tell them?"

They could use a combination of the things we learned. First, I'd look at creating an immediate annuity from whatever savings they have. For instance right now, if you are a 65-year old man, you could invest $100,000 in an immediate annuity and receive an annual income of about $7,848 or, if you're a woman, $7,392 a year. Not much but this is only the beginning.

Pat asked, "Would you delay receiving Social Security?"

"Right. I'd advise them, particularly the husband, to delay taking Social Security until age 66. Remember if a man delays, for instance, he could probably increase his income from Social Security by at least 25%–30%. This is huge."

"What would he live on in the meantime?" Charlie said.

"He could take money out of whatever savings he had. But like we talked about, if he thinks he'll live past his early 80's, then he should definitely delay taking the benefits."

"So now you've found two extra sources of income. Where's the third?"

"They could sell their home and buy-down in price to free-up some of their equity. That could be used for an immediate annuity, for instance, or at least it'll cut their overhead a lot. That means more money in their pockets. If this still isn't enough to support them, they could use a reverse mortgage. As you learned, they're expensive but if this is all they got going, I say use it."

"This sure is a 'go-for-broke' strategy," Pat said.

"Yeah, but if this is all you got, what can you do? It makes me sad when these people come in my office. I'd like to wave a magic wand and create savings where they have none, but I can't do it. I have to give them the best advice I can. Luckily, you folks aren't in that mess."

Pat said, "Maybe we should have spent more and enjoyed it?"

"Well…There are lots of people who save very little and then 'go for broke' as you say. The difference is, you folks have choices. Most of those others don't have any. You've got freedom. They don't. No matter how much or how little money you have, freedom's a wonderful thing to have. It's worth a lot more than money."

"I don't feel like that very often. I usually feel pinched because we're trying to be careful with how much we spend and save," Charlie said.

"I know. Everyone feels that way. But freedom from worry allows you to enjoy the present time because you're not wondering how you're going to pay for something tomorrow. That's a wonderful thought: to be free of worry and to enjoy wherever you are, whatever you're doing. Very few people get to that point. I guess to me, it means being satisfied with what you have and where you are at any given moment."

Working during Retirement

The fact is, that for many people, working during their "retirement" years is going to be a necessity. Simply put, they have not saved enough to create adequate income for themselves.

A study done by AARP in 2002 showed that 71 percent of workers age 45 to 56 plan to work into their retirement years. In addition, 18 percent planned to work mainly for the extra income. Others, planned to work for combined reasons of income, interests, and enjoyment. The idea that a person faced an either/or situation—either you work full time, or not at all, is changing.

When you also consider the decline in traditional pension plans and health care benefits, many people choose to work out of necessity for these reasons.

If you find yourself in this situation, are there ways to accommodate working and retirement at the same time?

There's good news for most people in this position. The opportunities and need for older workers continues to increase. Here are some suggestions if you're contemplating working after "retirement".

1. Talk with you present employer about the possibilities of working a flex schedule, reduced hours, working from home, staggered work loads, or some type of phased-in retirement.

2. Explore with your employer the possibility of using technology to make your job more flexible. This might allow working from home or the ability to use flexible work schedules or even some travel, while continuing to work and stay in touch with the office.

3. Look at chances to job share with other, older employees. Splitting one job between two people may be attractive to the employer because of reduced costs.

4. Consider re-educating yourself into a new area that is connected with your present skills, but different enough to lead to other work opportunities.

5. Look at ways to "free lance" your present skills for projects or part time work.

6. You could start your own business, particularly if you draw upon your present skills and network of friends and business associates.

Everyone agrees that some work after retirement is good for a variety of reasons. It keeps you healthy, both physically and mentally. For many, the opportunity to learn something new, meet new people, to feel valued, and to socialize with others, is well worth the extra effort.

And the extra income helps!

What my notes said

1. By starting a small business and incorporating it, which isn't hard to do, you can create another stream of income and also be able to deduct all kinds of expenses. This, too, creates more income for the work you do.

2. I encouraged Charlie and Pat to look at what they owned right now and see if there were any rental opportunities. A lake cabin, extra garage space, for instance, could be rented for a short time and the extra income would supplement other retirement income.

3. There are some "last chance" ways to create extra income using whatever cash savings people had. Immediate annuities could create a steady source of income. They could sell their house and buy down into a cheaper one. The equity they release could be invested to create more income, too.

4. For many, the necessity to work after retirement is going to force them to find something to do for extra income. There are many good reasons to do so.

Lesson Six:
Learn to give from your assets
and your life

Lesson Six:
Learn to give from your assets and your life

Chapter Thirteen

Become your own charity

"I find that the older I get, the less I think about my needs and the more I think about others' needs. There're so many opportunities all around us to help others," Charlie said.

"That's a good place to be. It's sad but I find that many people in retirement have a very different attitude."

"What's that?" Pat asked.

"Well, they feel like they've worked hard all their lives, saved and scrimped their money, and now they are entitled to relax, be self-indulgent, and spend it."

"What's wrong with that? Sounds kind of good to me."

"Of course it is but you didn't hear anything in that sentence about what they might offer to the community, did you? So often, their plans are all about themselves. I understand that they feel they've already given: to their employers, their families, their partners, their friends, to the government through taxes. I know. But look at it this way. Suppose a couple retires at 62 and lives until 87. That's twenty-five years of self-indulgence!"

"Yeah, I see your point. The way you put it, it almost sounds boring," Pat said.

"That's why I wanted both of you to think beyond money and look at the larger issues of what you want your life to be. It helps you focus on what you're really here for. For what purpose. I think it was Albert Einstein, when he was asked about the purpose of life, replied that 'of course, it is to serve others. What else could it be?' he said…did I tell you this before? I keep repeating myself these days. Sorry."

Pat turned silent and thought of something. Then she said, "I like golf and I like going out to dinner, vacations and all that but I gotta admit, something's been rattling around the back of my brain. Not since we were very young children, have either of us been 'on vacation' all the time. I wonder what it'll be like. It's a little unnerving, really."

"Yeah," Charlie nodded. "Funny, but I've been thinking some of the same things. I know a number of people who retired to travel and relax and they turned into alcoholics! It kinda bothers me too."

"When you think about what most people have been through in their lives… Whether they're formally educated or not, all of us have been workers, foremen, teachers, coaches, parents. We've been through sickness, trouble, failures, and successes. To me, people at this stage of their lives, retirement that is, have so much to offer. Most people have developed <u>wisdom.</u> This is different from being educated or even smart. I mean that they've learned a lot about living through this Life, good and bad. And that knowledge is valuable…too valuable to let it sit without being used or offered to the community."

Charlie asked, "Are you talking' about volunteering?"

"Of course that may be part of it. It's the immediate reaction of many people. No…I'm talking about something much broader. More of an attitude, I think. Volunteering may be something that fits for you or Pat. But it doesn't always fit for others. That's okay. The possibilities for contributing are just being discovered. It can become a challenging, creative pursuit."

"Where should we start?"

"Well, family seems like the place to start, for me," I said. "We could consider this in two directions: to those younger than you and those older. Your kids and grand kids or elderly parents. I'm sure any of them could use help. And unlike most other contributions to the community, usually a family knows best what each one needs. You can control more carefully, the outcome of giving your money or efforts. For each direction, there are different strategies and advantages."

"Can we talk about kids? We don't have any grand kids yet, but we may as well include them, too. Sounds like the ideas you have would fit both?" Pat said.

What a lot of people don't realize, is that it's very easy and not too expensive to create a sizable benefit for kids/grand kids. You've got two, old tools that'll give you a lot of power: time and compound returns. I think it was Einstein again, who said that compound interest was the greatest invention of Mankind.

Here's a simple example. Suppose you gave $10,000 worth of mutual funds to a child as a gift. You'd avoid paying gift tax since a parent can give up to $11,000 a year without triggering a tax. You also made monthly contributions to the funds in the amounts of $50 or $75. We'll assume the funds grow at 8% a year after taxes. Here's what your child would have.

Years	$50	$75
5	$18,522	$20,334
10	$31,294	$35,842
15	$50,321	$58,947
20	$78,669	$93,370

"What if we don't have twenty years with each child to let this grow?" Pat asked.

If there are only ten years before the child needs the money, you would still have $35,842. Which is better than nothing. Think of starting something like this when your first grandchild is born. Then, you may have thirty years or more.

Depending on the family, each one is different. But there are two areas that almost everyone wants to help with: education and future expenses, like a down payment on a house, or a big trip after graduation, for instance. There are lots of ways to do this.

"College funding…what a nightmare!" Charlie said.

For most people, it's difficult because they've never saved enough and when the time comes, they all struggle. Think how nice it would be to start a grandchild's fund when they're born. It'd help the grand kid and your children immensely.

Here are some strategies that work.

Direct gifts of money to children

This is the easiest solution. You set-up an account in the child's name and invest money into it. If the child's a minor, you could name yourself or the grandchild's parent as a joint tenant. If the money is registered in the grandchild's name, all income and capital gains earned by the account are taxed to the grandchild, at his/her tax rates. Wealthy people like this sometimes because it gets money out of their estates to save estate taxes.

"I don't know…" Pat said. "if my grand kids are anything like our kids now, I don't know if I'd trust them with the money. Can they get at it anytime?"

In most states, once the child turns 18, they have full control over it and can do **anything** they want with it. It's legally theirs.

"What if they're less than 18?" Charlie said.

Transfers to minors and trusts

There's always been the Uniform Transfer to Minors laws in most states. They are called UTMA's or Custodial Accounts. It's the same concept as we've covered before, except that an adult must be the custodian of the funds until the child turns 18. Then, they get full control. But even when a parent is a custodian, they must be very careful to protect the money for the child. They can't spend it on themselves, for instance.

"So you still end up with Pat's worry: the kids can take the money and run."

The other disadvantages are that once the money is put into the UTMA, the person giving the money cannot take it back. And since it becomes the property of the child, when they go to apply for financial aid for college, this fund becomes an asset of the child's that they have to declare for aid purposes.

Pat thought for a while. Then said, "I heard on the 'Oprah' show the other day something about setting-up trusts for grand kids and kids. Do you know anything about that?"

The parent or grandparent establishes something called an "irrevocable trust". It's irrevocable because once the money is put into the trust, the donor can't get it back.

They're not too complicated. It acts just like a separate person. Its terms are created by the person giving the money. So, for instance, the grandparent can dictate exactly when portions of the money can be accessed. Usually, people choose different ages like, 21, 35, 40, whatever. Someone has to act as a trustee to administer the trust and the money inside it. They're responsible for protecting the money. When you hear the jokes about rich kids living off their trust funds, this is what they're talking about. Because the donor can allow the grandchild to have a certain amount of income from the investments in the trust, also.

"That sounds pretty good to me. I mean, to protect the child from wasting the money too early." Pat turned to me. "Why didn't we set-up two of these for the kids?"

Once you put money into a trust, you can't get it back. And even if your lawyer prepared the papers and set it up, it's still expensive to administer. Remember that a trust acts just like a person. That means that under the law, the trust has to maintain records, pay taxes, and maybe pay fees for the management or administration of the trust. Unless you've got a lot of money to dump into something like this, they're expensive and may not be worthwhile. There are other, less expensive options a person could use to accomplish the same goal.

Giving to children through a Roth IRA

This is one of the best. Because the child can use it for almost anything he or she wants. Remember that the kid has to earn some money to set-up a Roth. But there's nothing that says the <u>child</u> has to fund it. Grandparents can fund it for the child. All the other rules apply: no distributions before 59 ½ without paying the 10% penalty unless the withdrawals are from the original investment amount. Once withdrawals are made, there's no income tax paid on them. The child has to wait for years before taking money out, you can imagine how much these funds could grow!

"There are a lot of parents who feel their children should wait to 59 ½…to be mature enough to handle the money." Charlie said.

Another possibility is for grandparents to name the grandchild as a beneficiary on their own Roth IRA. When the grandparent dies, the grandchild inherits the Roth. There's a little wrinkle. Even though there's normally no income tax assessed on withdrawals from a Roth, when someone inherits a Roth, they must begin making theRequired Minimum Distribution as if this was a regular IRA and pay income taxes on that amount. Of course, if the child is young enough, you spread it over their life expectancy so it won't be too much.

Use of permanent life insurance for children

"Are you gonna bring us back to the Variable Universal Life insurance we learned about a few weeks ago?" Pat asked.

This product is very flexible and can be used in many different situations. Here's how it works. Let's say your grandchild is five. You could take out a permanent variable universal life insurance policy on the child. The child could be the owner. You pay for the insurance and over fund the policy to build-up the investment portion of the cash value. Over the years, it grows tax-deferred and later, when the child needs some money, they can borrow from the policy in a tax-free situation. They also have a certain amount of insurance protection in case they die.

"This sound's better to me than the Roth because the kid can get at the money earlier, for college, for instance.," Said Pat.

"It's got that going for it. Do you recall one of the drawbacks for this type of insurance for you to invest in now?"

"Uh…it's probably going to be very expensive. Especially as we get older."

"Yes. But the costs of insurance for a five-year old is pennies. Once the policy is started, the premiums remain level for the rest of the child's life."

Charlie asked, "So are there any drawbacks to this strategy?"

When the child reaches 18, they can tap into the money and take-out whatever they want. If they take too much, they'll "bankrupt" the policy and it'll be cancelled. Unlike the inherited Roth, the child has the opportunity to get his or her hands on the money—for whatever reason they want to spend it on.

"Uumm," Pat nodded her head. "It's all very interesting. I s'pose we could use a combination of many of these ideas, couldn't we?"

"Of course. And we haven't even gotten to funding for college yet. For that specific purpose, you got more choices," I said.

Strategies for saving for college

Coverdell Savings Accounts and US Savings Bonds

Some people use an old favorite—US Savings Bonds. The grandparents buy the-bonds for the grand kids with after-tax money. The interest grows tax-deferred and if you use the proceeds for college expenses, it's tax-free. Interest rates on savings bonds are very low and the child can get control of the money to use it for things other then college. These are two of the drawbacks to using US Savings Bonds. However, for many people, the security of these is important. As with so many financial strategies, the choice of one or another depends on the comfort level of the investor. These bonds are not a bad way to save for college, but there are other tools that have more advantages.

There are also Education IRA's, that were limited to contributions of $500/child/year. In 2001, they were renamed Coverdell Savings Accounts and the maximum limit was raised to $2,000/child/year. They work by putting after-tax money into the account. It grows tax deferred, and any money withdrawn for education purposes is tax-free.

In addition to college expenses, these have the added advantage that you can use them for elementary and secondary schools also. To start one, you open it yourself and name a grandchild as the beneficiary. If that child doesn't use the money, you can change the beneficiary to someone else in the family.

Good as this may sound, they're rarely used. The maximum limit is only $2,000. Besides, the new 529 Plans are probably better. In fact, many financial institutions don't even offer the Coverdells. They are too much trouble to open, for too little money, in their opinion.

Are 529 College Plans a good deal?

"Dumb question: where does the number 529 come from?" Pat asked.

The number comes from the IRS code number. It's the newest tool we have and it's one of the best. There's been a lot of attention on these, with lots of advertising. They're set up by a parent or grandparent, although it could be anyone, for that matter, not even a family member. Technically, they're offered through each state but usually, the state will contract with a financial institution, like mine, to actually run the program. After-tax money is invested in the giver's name, with the grandchild named as the beneficiary. You have to set-up a separate one for each child.

The money inside the 529 grows tax-deferred, and any money coming out for college expense is tax-free. There are also other, important advantages.

1. The limit on maximum contribution per child per year is several thousands of dollars depending on the state. (Normally, a grandparent, for instance, can give up to $11,000 per child per year <u>without</u> triggering a gift tax. But there's a special exclusion—up to $55,000 can be invested in one year for each child without paying gift tax. The giver can't put in anymore for a five-year period but the advantage is that the investments will grow tax-deferred for five years. And—each grandparent can put in $55,000 for each beneficiary)

2. The definition of "college expenses" is very broad: tuition, books, room and board, computers if used for educational purposes, educational travel, etc.

3. If the beneficiary child receives a scholarship, for instance, and doesn't need the money, the givers/owners can take the money out without penalty or can simply change the name of the beneficiary to anyone else in the extended family—not limited to a child. So if the wife of a giver wants to go back to school for a master's degree, her name can be substituted.

4. The giver's the owner and can always get the money back. There would be some penalties but at least, they keep control over the money. This is a huge factor for some people.

5. Some states give a state income tax deduction for contributions to a 529 plan offered by that state.

6. For financial aid purposes, the US Department of Education has stated these accounts won't be considered an asset of the child—therefore they won't count against the child's eligibility for student aid. Another big concern for many people.

Here's a chart comparing all three vehicles.

Comparing College Savings Plans

	529 Plan	Coverdell Savings	UTMA
Who controls the money	Owner	Owner	Transfers to Child age 18
Can you change Beneficiaries	Yes	Yes	No
Taxation of Account earnings And withdrawals	Federal income tax deferred. Withdrawals tax-Free for education	Same as 529	Earnings taxed At child's rate Withdrawals not taxed

Maximum yearly Contribution	Varies by state Can be as much As $187,000/yr.	$2,000/yr	$11,000/yr without paying Gift tax
Investment options	Wide range of Securities	Same	Same
What can you use Proceeds for?	Any accredited Post secondary School	K-12 and post secondary school	Any use
Penalties for non-Qualified withdrawals	10% penalty on earnings	Same	No
Ownership of assets Counted for financial Aid purposes	Account owner	Student	Student
Age restrictions	None	Can't be made After 18	Account transfers to Child at 18
State tax deductibility For contributions	Some states allow	No	No

"How's the money invested inside the 529?" Pat asked.

Most companies offer a family of mutual funds to choose from. The actual choices are tilted toward more aggressive funds for younger beneficiaries and are shifted to more conservative funds as the child gets nearer to starting college and will need the money.

The drawbacks to 529 plans include the costs of administration of the plan and the mutual funds are a consideration The biggest drawback is that once the money is invested into the 529 Plan, it must be used for educational purposes only. You can change the beneficiaries but it must still be used for educational purposes to avoid taxes and penalties. And with the lower tax rates on income that Congress has passed, the tax-shelter effect of 529 Plans decreases. For some people, the freedom of use and lower fees in taxable accounts is actually a better deal.

Pat asked, "Would you be more careful in picking mutual funds for a taxable account?"

"Not necessarily more 'careful' but I'd choose funds or investments that generated <u>low tax consequences</u>. Municipal bonds or funds that created a lot of dividend income, for instance."

"So, if a grandparent wanted to help with a down payment on a house, let's say, the 529 Plan wouldn't work?"

When people are planning to give, it's a good idea to look at a combination of strategies. They're not limited to just one. Depending on the age of the child, if the giver wants to keep control, how much money is given, and the tax consequences, we can use a variety of options. Each situation will be different. But that's the beauty: they can design something to fit each person's needs and still accomplish what's most important. The giving of something; in this case, money.

Start a Business

"Remember when we talked about the advantages of starting your own business and setting-up a small corporation?" I said.

"Of course. There are all the expenses you can deduct <u>before</u> you report your net, taxable income,"

"Last time, we focused on the financial benefits but there are many other opportunities that small businesses offer."

"I can imagine," Pat said. "I know many middle-aged people who've either retired or been downsized and laid-off that started their own business. Most of my friends like that are happy. They tell me they sometimes work harder but they like the freedom and control over their work lives."

One of the hardest things about starting a new business comes when the owner needs the income to live on. They don't have any other sources of money to support their families while the business grows. When people have retired, typically they have other sources of income. It enables them to weather the early years when sales and incomes are starting to grow and frees them to pursue other opportunities.

For instance, they can choose a product or service that they truly love. It may not be as lucrative but it can be something they really have a passion for. And that comes back to our lesson today, about giving.

"I suppose they could volunteer for something," Pat said.

"Well, sure but I'm thinking in larger terms. Why not pick a business which has the specific purpose of helping someone?"

Pat said, "I just read about a small business company in France that's developed a cheap, simple food product that they sell in Africa to relief groups. It's kind of like peanut butter, loaded with nutritious value, that comes in a tube like toothpaste. Is that what you mean?"

"Right. There are so many needs—many of them right here. If you sell in Africa, great. But there's lots of need here, too. Volunteer work is always wonderful but I've found that when someone is running a business, the effort, attention, and the outcome can be multiplied many times. If you volunteer Pat, you're only one person contributing. But if you start a business, now you can employ others or contract with others and multiply all your efforts. Not only do you create a product or service, but you also create jobs for others.

Now, we'll go a step further. We said it'd be a good idea to pick a product or service that directly helps people. I suppose all products 'help' people somehow, but I mean something like the food company in France that Pat mentioned. Why not think bigger and purposely employ the types of people who normally don't have the opportunities for good jobs that most others do. Maybe elderly, disabled, or poor. See what I mean? How one small business can do a tremendous amount of good in the world?"

"Yeah…I got a friend from the Army who runs a small metal manufacturing company. He doesn't purposely hire poor, recovering alcoholics but it seems he has many on the payroll. He understands how difficult it is for them so he bends over backwards to keep them hired. They have to do the work, of course, but he really supports them in many ways besides just the job."

"The job itself is a tremendous thing to give someone," Pat said.

"See how creative and important this can become? By targeting a charitable need in the community, you can do an awful lot of good—and still make some money in your retirement!"

"I've got an idea," Pat said. "Lots of small businesses sponsor charitable events. Like runs for breast cancer, fund-raisers, music festivals and things like that. Not only does it give the business a high profile and lots of publicity, it's really helping something important."

The idea of giving is really an attitude to be developed. It can become a way of life, particularly in the years after you've been freed from working for someone else. So many people have been so blessed with so many things. Try to plan for a big part of your efforts to go toward giving. Many aspects of work involve giving—sometimes for pay, sometimes not. Each day, look for opportunities to give to those around you in even the smallest ways.

"One of the most important things I've found to give is my time," Pat said. "So often when we're working long hours at a career, we're busy and don't seem to have much time. But especially after retirement, the pressure of working and deadlines and projects that need to be completed, disappears. I'm finding that just taking the time to listen to people is so helpful to them."

"It comes back to my idea that giving is an attitude. A conscious, daily effort to find helpful, creative, and fun ways to give something of yourself. Let me give you an example of something that works for me. As you know, I love to play music and my saxophone," I glanced at them. "As it turns out, there are dozens of opportunities to play for others. For a musician, performing is one of the highlights of the whole process. Of course, I get paid often but some of the most satisfying gigs have been those we did for fund raisers and charitable groups. Think of how great this is: I'm giving something important to others and having the time of my life doing it!"

What my note said

1. Einstein's quote that the **purpose of living was to serve others** provided the bedrock for all the suggestions I offered them.

2. I started by looking at ways to give to family:

    a. **Direct gifts** of money to members. Saves on costs but gives control of the money to the person receiving it. May also trigger taxes depending on how large the gift

    b. I taught them about **Custodial Accounts** where money is given to children, taxed at their rates, but administered by an adult. Lots of people don't like this idea because control of the money goes to the child at some point.

    c. Some parents and grandparents use **Roth IRA's** as a way to give money. It ties-up the money until the child is 59 ½ (withdrawal without penalty) but has the advantage of forcing the child to let the growth run for many years, creating a huge asset in their later lives. Of course, the proceeds from a Roth are never subject to income tax

d. Another strategy is to invest in **Permanent Life Insurance**, like a Variable Universal Life policy and to over fund it above the cost of the insurance premiums. It works like a Roth but has the advantage of higher contribution limits and, of course, provides the child with life insurance. It's biggest disadvantage is the cost, which is much higher than a Roth IRA

3. I showed them ways to **give for College Savings**

   a. They could contribute to a **Coverdell Savings Account.** It grows tax deferred and is tax-free if the proceeds are used for education expenses, including elementary and secondary schools. The limits on the investments are quite low compared to other resources, so these products aren't too popular.

   b. **US Savings Bonds,** although very conservative with low interest rates, are attractive to those looking for safety and security.

   c. **529 Savings Plans** are very popular and offer many advantages. The giving limits are high, the money grows tax-deferred, and can be withdrawn tax-free for education expenses. The giver retains control of the money also. The disadvantage is that once the money is put into a 529 Plan, it has to be used for education purposes only.

   d. **Permanent Life Insurance** can be used like a 529 Plan with the added advantage of not being limited to education expenses. A child could use the money for a down payment on a house, for instance. The disadvantage is the high cost.

4. I showed them the opportunities involved in **starting a Small Business** not only as a way to make money in retirement but as a way to give in unique and creative ways to those around us.

I reminded them that giving should become an **attitude of life**, a **daily habit** especially since most retired people have lots of things of value they could share and give.

Lesson Seven:
Learn to live a life of fulfillment

Lesson Seven:
Learn to live a life of fulfillment

Chapter Fourteen

Re-thinking Success, Fulfillment, and Life

I met with Pat and Charlie for one, last meeting. I had given them all the tools I had to help them decide if they could quit working and what to prepare for if they did. The weather had burst into the heat of summer. Thick, moist air tried to penetrate the coolness of my office. When they arrived, I could see the humidity in the sheen on their faces.

"Our meetings are coming to an end," I told them as we sat in our familiar chairs around the well-worn table. "Tonight, we'll learn the Seventh Lesson and after that, you've got the resources to do it on your own!"

"Your lessons have opened our eyes to many things we hadn't even thought to question. Problems we didn't even know were looming. But thanks for all the lessons; you're right. We feel well prepared now," said Pat. "Still, can we answer the question: When can we quit? When can we retire?"

"You've learned the financial lessons. There's one more—maybe the most important one in order to answer your question. We'll learn about Living a Life of Fulfillment."

"Aren't we gonna talk about money anymore?" Charlie asked.

"Yes and no. Having enough money and making decisions so that you don't have to worry about it certainly makes life a lot more fulfilling. But I want to go to the next step. You start with a good point. Because we are a society that seems to obsess about money…or more accurately, things. Lots of people look at retirement as a time to stop and savor their success."

"Well, yeah, that's just about everybody I know," said Pat.

"That's okay and can be part of retirement but notice two things:

1.   It creates an "end" where a person looks <u>back</u> at their success

2.   People think they should be seeking success—-when they really should be looking for fulfillment."

Many retired people, even if they've never spent a minute considering it, are looking back over their working years. Wondering if they've been "successful" in their job and lives. But success is the wrong thing to focus on for people who are retiring. For some reason, we have all been programmed to look at our life's work on a continuum.

We see failure at one end and success at the other end.

Failure—————————————————————Success

People work hard all their lives to get as far as they can to the right, to achieve success.

Pat interrupted, "That's not always bad. I mean, we need ambitious people to achieve and build new things in the world."

"Absolutely, I agree. And competition is vital to that. In some ways, the 'rat-race' really pushes people to accomplish tremendous things. As I see it though, success is usually external. It's represented and measured by things like income, power, rank, possessions, houses, athletic wins, and social standing. These are great but they're all outside of us. I meet with many, many successful people who are miserable. How can you explain that? Do you know people like that?"

Charlie said, "Particularly, in my business, there were more than enough over-achievers who were successful. At the same time, I always thought that as a group, engineers were more unhappy than others. In fact, a peculiar thing happened over and over. As people in my company made more money, they bought more things, got bigger houses, joined country clubs, and became 'more successful'. But the result was more work and less enjoyment of life. They were proud of the things and success that they could bring to their families but still remained unhappy with themselves and their lives."

The explanation is to realize that success is something entirely different then fulfillment. In fact, fulfillment is on a different plane or dimension from the Failure/Success continuum.

What does "fulfillment' mean, then?

For many, it's a sense that life is full, complete, that it's whole, secure, peaceful, and joyful. Happy…not always. But they do have a deep, consistent joy in their lives. It doesn't really have anything to do with success. In fact, it's often just the opposite.

Pat nodded. "Umm. I agree. I think there are more women than men who would agree with you."

"Probably. Women have not had the opportunities for material success that men have had so I suppose, they've thought about other, inside issues that men often ignore. I think men are trained early to compete for success and it gets reinforced from the locker room to the classroom. Then, in jobs, it just continues. The interesting phenomenon I've seen lately, is that as more women joined the upper ranks, they too, began to strive for the same outside measures of success, just like men."

"If we agree that fulfillment is something different from success and that we want to feel fulfilled, then how do we get it?" Charlie said. "We're really asking the fundamental questions of—Who am I and Why am I here?"

"Yeah, but beyond feelings of wholeness, can we be more specific about what we can do to be fulfilled?" Pat asked.

Creative and Meaningful Work

"We all work, of course. But most of us don't even like our jobs. Have you ever noticed that? Why do we say, 'Thank God it's Friday?'"

"Well, lots of people have difficult, stressful jobs. You can't ignore that," said Pat.

"Sure. I understand. The majority of people, in fact, have difficult often boring jobs to do. But maybe we should expand the walls…look at a job as something different than our work. Most of my clients feel that they were put on earth to do something meaningful, something important if even in a small way. Do you agree?"

"Yeah…"

"Joseph Campbell, the famous teacher of mythology, found that people the world over actually <u>want</u> to work. That is, they want to do something important in their lives. And it should be interesting or creative."

"I've been looking for that for years," Pat said.

"Here's the funny thing I've noticed," I continued, "the jobs that tend to be valued are those that are hard to do and are hard to learn." I looked at them and nodded. "And for most of us, if we learn something difficult and hard, we feel very successful, right?"

"Try becoming an engineer. Talk about difficult to learn, hard, and boring all at the same time." Charlie laughed and paused. "Come to think of it, why did I do it?"

Think of the things you do every day that are easy…that you never really had to learn because they just seemed to come from inside of you. Maybe it's your ability to hit a golf ball, or cook, or listen to people, or to make people happy, or to organize human or technological events. Perhaps it's an ability to lead people, make them feel calm, and to get them to trust you. Honest marital relationships and honest friendship are so valuable. These things you do are your **talents.** Most of us don't even recognize that we have them because they're so easy to do. But these are the gifts that each one of us have.

"I remember my favorite teacher in high school, telling me to 'do what I love' when I asked her for career advice," Pat said. "Maybe that's what she meant. But then, lots of things get in the way: like what your parents and friends and circumstances push you toward. I used to hear all the time, 'How can you expect to make a living at that?'"

That's the hard part: we have to support ourselves. This is the importance of expanding the walls around your "job" to include work. Jobs come and go. But your work, your purpose, can be permanent. If you tie your talents to what you do, you'll have important and creative work to do in the world. Sometimes, it may even happen in your job, but not always.

"So you say we should examine ourselves and recognize our talents, then use them in some positive way?" Charlie said.

"Yes. There are dozens of opportunities all around you to work with your talents to accomplish something important for someone else."

"I may still keep my job?"

"If you have to…But if you're not using your talents now, after retirement you have a brand-new opportunity to stretch your talents into meaningful work. Let's look at the second road to fulfillment."

Relationships

This is probably very obvious to most people. Relationships are vitally important. But I really mean something more. So often, we look at the idea of family or friends as something that <u>we</u> need in our lives. Stories are endless about the busy professionals or business people who work so hard they neglect their families. And the problem comes to rest with the narrow life lived by the individual. Men, in particular, have been urged to work hard and make lots of money for the family. Even if they're not around the family, if they provide for the material and luxury wants of the family, they're considered successful.

"Lots of women subscribe to the same idea," Pat reminded me.

That's a good example. If you can become a good and effective parent, you've probably achieved more than the majority of people have. But our culture doesn't reward that very often. Here's a great "revolutionary" idea: Why not care more for others instead of obsessing about yourself? Go into any bookstore and I bet about twenty-five percent of the books there are about "<u>self</u>-improvement"!

"It's interesting you said a while ago that we should look at the questions of who are we and why are we here? But it seems that the answers to these questions aren't found within ourselves," Pat said. "They're found outside of us. When we focus on how we can help those around us."

"Yes and I'm going to challenge you to make a 'game' of looking for ways to help on a daily basis. Make it fun. Have you heard of the 'Law of Compensation?'"

They both shook our heads.

"It simply says that if we make a practice of trying to help others, to give, that we will be compensated ourselves. It may not be money or even anything directly from the person we helped. But we will be rewarded. I use the term, 'Living Generously' to encourage and remind you."

"Sure," Pat said, "because, if nothing else, we'll feel fulfilled!"

"The third road deals with adversity. As they say, 'Stuff Happens'. How do we handle the ups and downs that life throws at us all the time?"

Controlling Attitudes and Feelings in the Face of Adversity

"But lots of bad luck happens to people in the world. We can't control that and for many of them, it's devastating," Charlie said. "Are you teaching us to 'think positively' all the time?" He waited for a response. "Because I don't agree. Just thinking positive won't change the bad things that happen to us all."

"Of course not. In fact, I'd go even further than you. I think there's very little that I have control over in this life. As humans, we get arrogant with our inventions and technology but in the end, there's actually very little we can control. Stuff happens. Some of it is 'good' for us but a lot of things are 'bad' for us." I paused and then smiled. "It's not what happens to us, it's how we react to what happens."

"Huh? If it's something bad, I can tell you how I'd react!" Charlie said.

"Remember weeks ago when we learned about the mental 'maps' that all of us carry with us? The maps that we've created to deal with the environment around us. Depending on what happens to us, we react to it."

"And lots of times those maps are old and out-of-date," Pat said. "So we react in the same old ways."

"Most people spend their lives trying to control the environment around them——and become very frustrated and depressed by the effort. We really can't control much of the things around us. What we can control, is <u>our response to the environment.</u> We can **choose** how to react."

"So, in the face of adversity, we can pick and choose what to do," Pat said.

"Yeah. Not only our behavior but our attitudes also. Our feelings. Reactive people let circumstances affect how they feel. An argument or rainy weather or an empty checking account, makes them feel horrible all day. But you see, they **choose** to feel this way. By default, they've chosen to give circumstances the power to dictate their attitudes and feelings. I'm suggesting that each of us has the power within us to choose not to feel this way."

"But what if one of your best friends dies? Grief isn't something I can simply 'choose' not to feel," Pat said.

Of course not. Then again, grief, although it hurts, isn't necessarily bad. Particularly if you come out of it with some growth for yourself. People who choose how they're going to react don't depend on their feelings, circumstances, or their environment to give them meaning and fulfillment. Instead, they choose their reactions based on their values and what is ultimately important to them. Difficulties will still happen to us all but if your value is to spend your time finding ways to help other people, then whether it's a rainy day or the bus was late, doesn't make as much difference to you. It's true freedom…the freedom to choose how we react to things and, ultimately, how we live. It does not mean that we just float along in life like a cork bobbing on the water. We may be more fulfilled by choosing our reactions but can we ever accomplish positive things?

"The ironic thing about this attitude is that as we choose our responses to circumstances, we actually end up changing some of the circumstances!"

"How does that work?"

"Each of us has our talents. When problems occur, we can direct our talents to trying to solve something about the problem. We can choose to not let the problem discourage us. We choose to try and fix the problem. If we can't, we can choose once again, to not let that stop us completely."

"Give us an example," Charlie said.

"Martin Luther King is a good one. In the face of seemingly intractable problems, he chose his reaction to the problems. It was different that the reactions of thousands of other people. He had a new road map in his mind. The power of his reactions, attitudes, and behavior toward discrimination and violence, changed the problems themselves."

Pat said, "all of these ideas sound wonderful: freedom, choice, self-control, fulfillment. So why don't more people live this way?"

"I think they're four things that hold people back."

Are your afraid?

There are all kinds of fear that each of us has inside.

1. **Fear of Failure**. I must succeed or I won't be a full, complete, successful person. This actually becomes worse as we get older. We become more cautious and seem to have "more at stake" as we age. It's one thing to "goof-up" at ten. It's another thing to goof-up at 62. Somehow, our egos get tied-up in our activities and thoughts, meaning that any failure becomes a direct blow to our sense of self-worth.

2. **Fear of Being Wrong**. We avoid situations where we may have our thoughts, opinions, or conclusions challenged. We worry we may not have the answers and especially as we get older, we're "supposed to know" the answers.

3. **Fear of Being Rejected**. We all have a powerful need to belong. Whether it's with a special group at work, on the golf course, neighborhood, or church, we abhor being left out. As a result, we often settle for far less just to avoid the risk of being excluded.

4.   **Fear of Emotional Discomfort.** We avoid situations where we may be embarrassed, vulnerable, not sure of ourselves, not in complete control, or we may make a mistake. It's tough to purposely push yourself into a situation where you aren't comfortable. As we age, it gets harder because for years, we've often had to be uncomfortable—in jobs, relationships, sports. Now, as we retire, we feel like we've been challenged enough; now is the time to relax by being in comfortable situations.

I said to Charlie, "If we're all full of these fears, why do anything? It's really tough to confront these. Believe me! I'm scared to death about playing the sax in front of an audience at the club. I've got all four fears about that!"

The path to fulfillment requires us to reject comfort and to do what might be uncomfortable, new ways of thinking and acting. But what's the alternative?

Lots of retired people seem active—golfing, going to lunch, fishing, traveling, puttering in the garden, working part time. Were they all unhappy?

I prompted them, "What's the opposite of growth? What do you see the plants outside going through now?"

"Well, decay, I guess. The plants die or hibernate over winter."

"Right. And so do we. We'll probably be very comfortable but we'll 'start to rust'. But to me, growth means growing up and going as far as I can with my talents. I was put here, now what can I become—starting from any age?"

"And retirement gives us a perfect 'break' in our lives and routines to try this."

"Yeah. If we choose to grow, we must choose to face our fears and push to our limits. Don't try to do what you know you can't do, but it does mean trying something you aren't sure you can do."

"I think I understand," Pat said. "I remember things I've tried that I wasn't sure about what I was doing. Was it gonna work? I didn't know for sure. But then, when I succeeded, I felt great! It was almost intoxicating—-like there was a larger, more complete, more in control of myself, 'me'."

"That's what I'm trying to get you to catch. When you push through your fears—and most of them are only in your mind anyway—you feel wonderful. You've got to become comfortable being uncomfortable. To practice a daily life of living at our own edges. That's where we discover our fulfilling life. It's where we feel the most excited or worried, passionate, alive, and worthwhile. It creates those rare moments when we feel like pumping our fist into the air and yelling, 'Yeah!!'"

"Do you mean we should all take big risks and start climbing mountains?" Charlie said.

Each person has their own fears, talents, and challenges. For some, it may be moving to Santa Fe, starting a small business, and learning how to snow board! For others, it may be pushing themselves to pick up the phone and call someone they've been meaning to get to know. Each of us faces different opportunities. The funny part about all this is that the more you push yourself into uncomfortable things, the easier it becomes to do it. Crazy as it sounds, you become 'comfortable' being 'uncomfortable'!

"And all the while you're growing," Pat said. "Or, as you said, we're growing-up to become the full person we were intended to be."

Creating Your New Life

"What should we do?" Charlie said. "What concrete steps can we take starting today?"

"It starts with your mind. The most powerful thing you have. The mind can create almost anything you want. If you can put the resources you already have—the creative and constructive power of your mind—to work, that will determine everything that happens to you. Thoughts are creative and they have the power to create a new reality for you. You become what you think."

"I don't know…" Charlie said.

"Let's look at the saxophone. I started playing that when I was forty-five. I'd never touched one before. But with a lot of hard work and effort to push my fears aside, I've come to the point of playing it regularly in a group. All our actions and behavior starts with the mind—the thoughts and dreams that we <u>can</u> do it."

"But when we retire, how do we start?" Pat said. "Facing the fears we have inside ourselves is the hardest thing to do."

"Who do you want to become? Who do you want to help? How will you do it? What activities with others give you the greatest feelings of self-esteem and pride? What things give you the greatest feelings of importance? From these answers, you can create a vision/dream of what is possible for you rather than where you're stuck now."

"It sounds tough. Those are big questions," Charlie said. "I would guess that most people procrastinate when it comes to facing them."

I nodded. "Of course—we're all human. That's why retiring is such a good motivation. We have the opportunity to change our lives. The last time that presented itself was probably in our early twenties. The difference now, is that we're all a lot wiser. Push past the self-doubts. We already have plenty of resources inside of us."

Pat said, "It's scary...well, uncomfortable like you said, but at the same time, it's exciting to think about the possibilities."

"It'll always be a combination of both. But when you get used to those two feelings, inside you at the same time, it gets easier. And you become much more fulfilled."

Exercises to Create a New Life

1. Catalog your values and talents

After you've answered personal questions that grow out of your dreams, begin to examine the values and talents you possess. The discovery of these will lead you in the direction that'll allow you to become the person you should be and want to be. You'll naturally lean toward those activities or work that make the most use of your talents. In addition, the cataloging of your talents will support your self-confidence in order to carry you through the barriers of fear.

2. Eliminate negative emotions

Start to eliminate the negative emotions of anger, blame, envy, resentment, self pity and fear. As humans, these types of feelings creep up on us every day. Make it a point, when you feel these negative emotions, to sweep them from your mind. Ignore them. They sap your energy and defeat you. Everyone is afraid of something. Find the courage to act in spite of fears, discomfort, and negative emotions. Turn your mind to a positive activity: when faced with negative emotions or problems, look at what you can do to solve the problem or eliminate the negative emotion.

3. Choose to be an active creator of your new life

As you push the negative emotions into the back round, that doesn't mean problems and changes will also stop. The difference is to avoid being passive about the things that happen around you every day. Resolve to view problems, setbacks, and changes as <u>opportunities</u> to learn and, therefore, grow. Make this a daily habit that when faced with a problem or difficulty, your first response should be to examine it for what good you can get out of it. Even negative events contain lessons that can teach us something.

4. Establish goals

As you discover which talents that you can draw upon for a new direction in your life, set-up goals for yourself. Many people think that the act of writing down goals is too confining, that a person loses their "freedom" to react to events by being tied to goals. Just the opposite is true. Goal-setting frees you to pursue many of the dreams you have. Without the goals, you lack direction and a plan to get your dreams. What kinds of goals should you set? Ask questions such as:

Where do I want to be in 10 years?

What do I want to be doing in 10 years?

Who do I want to have helped and how?

What will my life look like?

What things will I have accomplished or completed?

Once your goals are written down, you can determine the weekly steps you need to take to reach the goals. It'll give you the motivation to work at them.

Particularly, when faced with fears and doubts, you can focus on your goals and imagine how good you'll feel when you've accomplished them.

5. Be prepared to change—again and again

Just because you start to accept change and newness as part of your daily living, doesn't mean that's it forever. Changes keep happening. Be prepared for them and realize they contain all the necessary ingredients for new opportunities and fulfillment. Banish the word "failure" from your vocabulary. There's no such thing as failure—just an activity that didn't work. You learn from what didn't work and alter your plans and activities. Eventually, they will work.

What my notes said

1. Do we want success or fulfillment? There's a big difference and most people choose success

2. Fulfillment comes from five things:

   Creative and meaningful work

   Finding and using our talents to their full measure

   Discovering how we could strengthen our relationships by giving and helping others

   Controlling our attitudes and feelings in the face of adversity

   Overcoming our many types of fears–that each of us have

3. We can create a new life for ourselves by:

   Cataloging our values and talents

   Eliminating negative emotions regularly

   Choosing to be an active creator of our lives

   Establishing goals to work toward

   Being prepared to change–again and again

I put the cap back on my green pen and pushed back from the table. "I'm going to leave you two with a story about Thomas Edison. For me, it sums-up what retirement should be for everyone."

By late in his life, Edison had worked for years in his laboratory at Menlo Park. Years of research, experiments, and notes, representing almost a quarter century of his intense work, filled the lab in every corner. Unfortunately, a fire broke-out one night and destroyed most of the lab and, of course, its contents. The entire neighborhood came out to see the disaster that happened to this famous man. As the fire subsided, it appeared that everything was lost. A reporter found Edison near the smoking ruins. He was smiling!

The reporter couldn't believe it. All around him, people shook their heads in sympathy and despair. But there was Edison, smiling.

When the reporter asked him why, Edison responded, "I know it's all burned-up. But don't you see…all my mistakes are gone now. I can start again with a fresh mind and new ideas, unburdened by the mistakes of the past. I'm free to start over—how wonderful!"

Chapter Fifteen

So, When Can I Quit?

I've introduced you to several strategies, throughout the book, to help you answer this question. The focus has been primarily on financial concerns that you will face along with solutions to help you avoid the largest pitfalls. The decision to quit working involves so many other considerations beside the numbers, I also included ideas for the personal issues you will face.

That's because in today's world, even though we think of money as the <u>thing</u> we trade for all the other <u>things</u> we want, it's effect really goes a lot deeper. This is obvious when I talk to people and they tell me their "feelings" about money.

It makes them extremely uncomfortable. They run from it. Some obsess about it daily. Many work very hard to get it. People ignore it. People worry about it all the time, even if they have enough. Lots of people waste it. Some of my clients dream about it. A few feel guilty about it.

We all know the strong emotions that money can influence like power, security, confidence, fear, worry, happiness, and even a sense of comfort.

With this in mind, I started the book by challenging people to first decide what is fundamentally important to them in their lives. Put the issue of money and having enough of it, aside while you explore the bedrock purpose of your life. This sounds like an obvious practice, but I've found that many people look at the numbers first, then decide what they can "afford" to do after they retire. I'm suggesting a novel way to approach the question of quitting by focusing first on what kind of life do you want. What is truly meaningful to you? Which people are the most important in your life?

This is putting the "horse before the cart."

It's probably an exercise we should all go through early in our lives but, of course, most of us don't. Then, as work, families, expenses, hobbies, and all the pressures of daily life engulf us, we seldom have time to truly examine these questions. But when a person considers quitting work, this creates an ideal opportunity to look at these fundamental questions. It's also the perfect time to make the changes you discover you'd like to do.

When I was in college, there were posters that proclaimed, "Now is the first day of the rest of your life." I always dismissed them as sixties' rhetoric. Today, I understand the phrase and whole heartedly support it. More than ever, when you quit working, the rest of your life begins. Take advantage of it and make the most of it by thinking of what's important to you.

Once that exercise has yielded answers for you, the process of developing a financial plan that will support your new life, becomes easier. For one thing, it's focused now. You can calculate how much you'll need to support yourself. You can figure out how long you'll need income. Instead of spending your hard earned money on everything, you can aim it at the things you want to do with much greater efficiency and power. Your dollars will probably work harder for you than they ever have. You'll get control of your money and become organized about it. You'll be surprised at how effective you'll become at managing your money.

If you have painful memories about money or feel that you've wasted much of what you've had, a plan at this point, will enable you to move beyond those negative thoughts. Instead of worrying about money, you can direct your energy at positive thoughts of your money and how it's going to help you move to where you want to go and support you for a long time.

I stressed these principles in **Lesson One: Learn to raise your financial IQ.** When you learn how to protect yourself and to take advantage of coming financial opportunities, your life becomes easier. It's not hard but you must spend a little time learning these new principles.

The first question most people ask when thinking of quitting is, Will I have enough money to last? In **Lesson Two: Learn what new problems you'll face and how to Beat Them**, I cautioned you that three huge "wolves" are waiting to attack your money.

Inflation, the loss of purchasing power, is first.

We looked at the cost of postage stamps over a thirty-year period. You could look at almost any product or service and see the same thing. There's nothing to suggest that the dollar's relentless loss of purchasing power, will stop. When you quit working, you no longer have the protection of cost of living raises or promotions for more pay to enable you to maintain your purchasing power. If you don't maintain this, your life style will slowly, inevitably decrease year by year. I can tell you from the experience of people I've seen, it's very sad.

A variety of strategies could be employed. You could delay the decision to quit working, or delay in drawing from your retirement resources. By getting the money you have saved working harder, you can beat inflation.

The Avalanche of Taxes is second. We saw that there are several taxes that will have to be paid from your retirement income. Each of them alone is not too bad, but added together, they act like an avalanche and will fall on us with a combined fury. Most people have not made any provision for all the taxes they will have to pay. I have clients in their seventies who complain they're paying more in taxes than they earned fifteen years earlier.

To minimize taxes, you have to break up the combination of events that will occur and cause the heavy taxation.. Primarily, these are Social Security benefits, the Required Minimum Distribution rules affecting IRAs, pension income, and any other source of earned income you may have. Strategies include Roth conversions over a period of time and the use of insurance products which usually get favorable tax treatment. If you make careful, timed transitions of your money from taxable accounts to non taxable accounts, you can minimize these and put more dollars in your pocket.

Health care costs come in third, although for many people, this is a primary concern. Like inflation, there's no sign that these costs will stop growing. The projections are worse. There are various methods to try and reduce these costs from working with your employer to seeking groups that you can buy insurance through to get better rates.

It's important to remember that although you cannot eliminate these problems, with planning, you can minimize them to a great degree.

Lesson Three: Learn to stretch and grow–both you and your money–while reducing losses, introduced you to the idea that you can take charge of your money instead of worrying about it. You can change the maps in your mind regarding the way you view money and your life. The use of insurance to protect from risks like going into a nursing home and techniques to cushion economic downturns, can be implemented easily. This removes much of the worry about money and frees you to stretch and grow.

Today, we have sophisticated software programming to help you diversify your investments and to predict how long they'll last, through Monte Carlo models. All these strategies enable you to manage your money better and to quit worrying about it.

Lesson Four: Learn to get your money working harder for you, rather than you working harder for your money, gave you a variety of ways to power up your investments while keeping risk manageable. Asset Allocation models, rollovers of retirement accounts, reduction in taxes, all give your money more power. It's as important to learn how to minimize your losses in down markets, as it is to get the best growth in the up markets. There are easy ways to accomplish this.

I also explored different sources of income that you could look at. People generally depend on three sources of income for retirement needs: Social Security, pensions, and retirement accounts. I gave you techniques to maximize each of these. Most people simply accept the first number they're given without trying to increase the amounts. The creative use of insurance products can provide added income also while reducing taxes and giving more power to your dollars. You can take advantage of several of the tools you've already learned.

In **Lesson Five: Learn to create new sources of income for yourself**, I looked at unusual ways to get more income. Inheritances, annuities, using your home as a source of income, and starting a small business to take advantage of the benefits of that vehicle were explored. For many people, there will be the necessity of working after retirement. However, that is an ideal time to explore jobs or interests that are different or that really excite you and you've wanted to try for a long time. Not only is the extra income helpful (necessary) but you will learn and grow immensely.

In **Lesson Six: Learn to give from your assets and your life**, I moved to the idea that after we quit working, giving of ourselves is the ultimate reason for our existence. I offered many ways for you to give to your family and the community in effective and meaningful ways.

In **Lesson Seven: Learn to live a life of fulfillment,** I came back to the start of the book. I urged you to stretch, grow, overcome your fears, and create a life that, perhaps you only dreamed of living.

When people choose to quit working, I've seen them progress through three stages.

Stage One is the concern about money and if they'll have enough of it. Once this question is solved, they move onto the next stage.

Stage Two is engagement. This is a mental, emotional, and spiritual engagement with the people and world around them. Once people "find their place," they go a step further.

Stage Three is living the vision of giving back to the community. It takes the retired person out of his/her self. When this stage is explored to its fullest, I see the most joy and peace of any stage.

Perhaps, you're still wondering, When can I quit? I hope you see that this question can only be answered by you. I've tried to provide you with guidelines to use before and after you make the decision. You have the tools now. As Thomas Edison said after his lab burned, you can forget all the mistakes of your past and start fresh. What a thrilling idea!

I've included a checklist of items you should answer, or at least examine, before you make the decision to quit. A careful review of this checklist will lead you to your own answer

Checklist to answer the question

Do you have a plan?

You should start planning at least five years before you think you may want to retire. You'll be able to identify the critical issues for yourself and have time to prepare for them.

—Financial Plan—Determine the following issues

    How long will you money last

    Will you outlive your money

    Where will your sources of income come from

    Will your income be enough to beat inflation

    Have you insured against the financial risks you may face

    Have you planned to minimize taxes

—Personal Plan

    What do you plan to do next—work, travel, volunteer, play golf, etc.

    Where will you live Will you move for a few months a year

    What changes will you make in your life

    Who will you be with—family, new friends, new business people

Have you considered a "staged" retirement—while you tryout your new life plan

—Could you work part time at the same job

—Could you job share at the same job

—Is it possible to take some "leave without pay" for a few weeks/months and keep your job

—Do you have the opportunity to retire, collect a pension but work at the old job as a contract employee

—Is it possible to negotiate a severance package—cash bonus, pay for unused sick leave, establish a health care expense account, continue health care coverage

—Is it possible to reduce hours at work or work more from home

—Could you find a new job with more interest, less stress, part time, or in a more desirable area

—If married, what is your spouse going to do—could you coordinate your retirement plans/benefits

Have you checked on your pension benefits—if you're going to quit working completely

—How much will you receive

—Does it have inflation protection—if not have you taken that into account or planned to fight inflation with your other resources

—When would your pension start

—How do you get it started

—Have you met with your pension plan counselor

—Should you look at buying life insurance so you can get the maximum pension benefit—what's the cost of the insurance compared to the increase in your pension benefit

Have you checked on Social Security benefits—if you're going to quit

—What's the dollar amount of your benefit/spouse's benefit

—When is the best age to start collecting it for you

—How do you start it

—Have you met with any Social Security counselors to verify the accuracy of your information and to determine how to get the maximum benefit

–If your spouse has died, have you checked with Social Security to determine you benefits in relation to your spouse's earnings

–If you are divorced and were married at least ten years, have you checked with Social Security to find out what benefits you're entitled to and how to maximize them

Have you reviewed the most recent statement of all your other retirement benefits—401(K)s, Roth IRAs, IRAs, TSAs, etc.

—How much do you have in other assets

—Have you determined if you need to start taking money out now

—If so, how much will you need to take out—will your money last long enough

—Will you run out of money—do you have a plan to preserve it

—Should you convert your assets to a self-directed IRA

—Should you convert your IRA to a Roth IRA

—If yes, when is the best time to do this—how much should you convert

–Do you have a plan to coordinate these resources with others that you have, like pensions and Social Security benefits to provide adequate income for yourself

–Do you have a plan to make the best use of <u>all</u> your retirement resources

Have you planned for health care coverage in the "bridge" years to age 65

—Does your former employer offer this coverage

—If yes, how do you get access to it—what does it cover

—Should you work part time just to get health care coverage

—Can your spouse work to get family coverage for you too

—Is there a group that you could join to get the benefits of group rates if you have to purchase it on your own—what groups could you make use of—what do they offer—how much is the cost

Have you reduced your debt as much as possible

—You should have very little to no credit card debt

—Are there other debts you should pay off

—Should you pay off or pay down your mortgage—have you calculated the true cost of it

—Should you buy up to a more expensive house and take on more mortgage debt for larger tax deductions

Do you have a housing plan

—Should you stay in your home, move, buy-down to decrease debt

—What type of housing do you need

—Should you move to an area of your state or country that has a lower cost of living

—Should you live near or with family—children or parents

Have you prepared the legal plan

—Do you have a will with a list of assets/debts and their location

—Have you prepared a Living Will

—Do you need a Prenuptial Agreement

—Check the accuracy of all beneficiaries on insurance policies, pensions, IRAs, annuities, change them, if necessary

—If your assets are large, have you worked with an estate planning lawyer

—If you have charitable intentions for some of your money after you die, have you prepared for this—do the charitable groups and families know about your intentions

If you qualify for Medicare, have you

—Determined what your benefits will be

—Determined how to sign up for benefits

—Checked with an insurance agent about "medigap" insurance

—Where would you buy that and how much will it cost you

Have you checked on Long Term Care insurance

—What will it cost

—What benefits will you need and can you afford it

—Which company is the best one to buy from

—Should you make sure your policy premiums are tax-deductible

If you're going to Volunteer, what would you do

—Have you identified jobs or organizations that could use your help in a way that's interesting and productive for you

—Have you considered creating your own position within an organization to do something you really want to do

—Where's the best place for you to fully utilize your skills and talents

If you're going to Start a Business

—Have you identified a product/service for which there is a genuine need

—Is it something that will utilize your talents and skills

—Have you developed a business plan

—Will you incorporate

—How will you finance it

—How much time are you willing to devote to it

—How will you sell your product/service

Having fun!

–Do you have a plan to use your money and time for something that you really want to do

–Are you able to move into this stage of your life without worry

–Are you prepared to change many aspects of your life and do it willingly

If you would like to order more books or contact the author

www.iuniverse.com

1-800-288-4677 Ext. 501

Glossary

Annuity—Is a giant I.O.U. with an insurance company. The customer "lends" a sum of money to the insurance company and, in turn, they promise to pay it back in the future.

In the meantime, the customer's money has an opportunity to grow. Annuities also contain a Death benefit which means if the customer dies, his/her beneficiary will be guaranteed to receive nothing less than the original amount invested. Money that is inside an annuity will grow tax deferred. Annuities come in three main types.

Annuity-Immediate—A customer gives the insurance company a sum of money. In return, the company starts a life-time stream of income payments to the investor that are guaranteed to never decrease and never to end as long as the investor is alive. Once death occurs, if there is any money left in the annuity, it goes to the insurance company. On the other hand, if the investor lives longer than expected, he/she will continue to receive payments even if the annuity has run out of money.

Annuity-Fixed—A customer gives the insurance company a sum of money and it's invested by the company in a variety of instruments that give the customer a fixed rate of return, something like a Certificate of Deposit. Regardless of whether the stock market is rising or falling, these annuities will continue to grow at the pre-determined rate of return.

Annuity-Variable—A customer gives the insurance company a sum of money which is invested in the annuity in a variety of mutual funds. The growth of these funds varies with market conditions and growth is not guaranteed.

Asset Allocation—Is a term that refers to the spreading of risk among several types of investments. Typically, it is used in conjunction with a group of mutual funds to balance the different opportunities and risks. Several academic studies have created models for investors to follow to take maximum advantage of this strategy. It's sometimes referred to as "not putting all your eggs in one basket".

Beneficiary—Is the person, or institution, that will receive the proceeds of assets upon the death of the owner. Is also used in 529 College Savings Plans, even though the owner of the plan doesn't die, the recipient of the funds is called a beneficiary.

Beneficiary IRA—When the owner of an IRA dies before the IRA has been emptied, the person who inherits the IRA is called the Beneficiary and must set-up this special type of IRA which contains many advantages for the beneficiary and his/her own beneficiaries.

529 College Savings Plan—Is one of many tax-advantaged strategies available for college savings. The person who contributes to the plan is the owner and retains ownership of the funds. They are typically invested in a group of mutual funds within the 529 Plan. The beneficiary of the plan can use the money for college expenses. Growth of the money in the plan is tax-deferred and, if the proceeds are used for educational purposes, the money comes out tax-free also.

Coverdell Savings Account—Another strategy for college savings. These work similar to 529 Plans but have much lower contribution limits for the year. Once the 529 Plans became available, the popularity of the Coverdells dropped.

Deferred Compensation—Is a retirement account available to employees where pre-tax money is invested in a group of mutual funds to grow for retirement purposes. When the money is taken out, it is fully taxable and after age 70 ½, it must be taken out according to IRS rules. While the money is in the Deferred Comp retirement account, it grows tax-deferred however.

Diversification—A term that means spreading out a person's investments over several types of investment opportunities. The theory says this practice reduces risk and gives the investor the opportunity for potential growth in many areas.

Dividends—Companies will sometimes pay part of the profits earned during the year back to their stockholders. These payments are called Dividends. They are not guaranteed to be paid but when they are, they add value to the stock ownership in addition to the potential growth of the price of the stock itself.

Dollar Cost Averaging—An investment process where the individual invests the same amount every month, regardless of the movement of the market. The theory says that when the market prices are down, the investor automatically purchases a <u>greater</u> quantity of shares of mutual funds, at the lower price. When the market goes up, the investor automatically purchases a <u>smaller</u> quantity of shares at the higher price. It gives the investor the opportunity to buy more shares at lower prices in a simple, disciplined manner.

Equity REITS–These are mutual funds that invest in real estate opportunities and, therefore, are called Real Estate Investment Trusts. They operate under special IRS rules and securities rules but are sold like mutual funds. They give investors an opportunity to put their money in real estate investments in smaller amounts and with good diversification.

401(K)—Is a retirement plan offered by private companies. A third-party financial company sets-up the plan for employees. Both employees and employers may contribute. The employee contributes pre-tax dollars into a selection of mutual funds. They grow tax-deferred. When the employee retires, they may withdraw the money but will pay full state and federal income tax on the amounts they withdraw.

Growth Stocks—Stocks that are categorized as companies that have a good potential for growth in earnings and profits. This should translate into a rise in the price of the stock. Usually, these companies don't pay dividends so the investor is hoping that he/she will get a rate of return based solely on the rise in the price of the stock.

IRA—An Individual Retirement Account. It's a private account where a person can put in pre-tax money, invest it in a variety of ways within the IRA (Usually people use mutual funds within the IRA), the growth is tax-deferred until money is taken out. At that time, it's fully taxable. The advantage is the years of tax-deferral to allow the money to grow as much as possible. Withdrawal options are very flexible.

IRA Withdrawal Rules—See the Required Minimum Distribution entry

Life Insurance—A contract with an insurance company to pay a pre-determined death benefit to the beneficiaries of the policy when the insured dies. There are two types of life insurance:

Term Insurance–Is "temporary" insurance in that it only lasts for a certain period of time, typically 10,15, or 20 years—as long as the insured continues to make premium payments. At the end of the time, the insurance disappears and the person must apply again for coverage under a new policy. There's no build-up of cash value or investment opportunities. The biggest advantage is the fact it's much less expensive than permanent insurance.

Permanent Insurance–As long as the insured makes the premium payments, this type of insurance continues in effect until the insured dies. The insured also has the opportunity to put more than the premium into this vehicle and invest it, inside the policy, into mutual funds or fixed-income funds. The advantage is that the money grows tax-deferred within the policy and may be "borrowed" by the insured in a tax-free manner. There are no Required Minimum Distribution rules for insurance policies. The death benefit will be at least the pre-determined amount plus any growth that has occurred in the investment portion of the policy. Loans taken out previously, would be deducted from the death benefit.

Living Will—Is a "road map" prepared by a person to instruct others (Usually family) on how to handle the "end of life" questions and decisions. A common feature would be an instruction to not use extraordinary medical methods to prolong life, for instance.

Long Term Care Insurance—A type of insurance that pays a pre-determined daily dollar amount to the policy holder if they are unable to perform two of the six Activities of Daily Living, as defined by the company. The better policies allow the insured to use this money for nursing homes and, in addition, assisted care facilities, or home health care needs. They actually allow a person to stay our of a nursing home, as a result. The advantage is the insured doesn't need to use all of their other assets to pay for expensive care. On the other hand, these policies can be expensive.

Medigap Insurance–Insurance that "fills the gap" between what Medicare will pay for and what the retired person must pay out of pocket for services.

Monte Carlo Analysis—Computer generated model that is used for retirement planning purposes to try and answer the question of whether a person's money will last throughout the rest of their life and not run out. It's very sophisticated and supported by years of academic research. The results are expressed in probabilities—which is why the name Monte Carlo is used.

Money Market Funds—Are mutual funds that buy very short-term investments and, as a result, quite conservative. Unlike other mutual funds where the price of the fund rises and falls, Money Market Funds are always expressed as $1 a share. What rises and falls are the rates of return. Can be a good alternative to savings accounts or Certificates of Deposit.

Municipal Bonds—Are investments sold by municipalities such as cities, counties, etc. They are giant I.O.U.'s where the municipality borrows the money from investors and promises, in return, a growth rate. They are very stable and secure but the growth rates tend to be low. The big advantages to these are that the growth portion the investor receives is tax-free at the federal level and may be tax-free if the investor purchases bonds from municipalities in the state in which they live.

Mutual Funds—Are regulated companies that offer shares to investors for purchase. The money is then invested in a variety of stocks and bonds, depending upon the purpose for the fund. (Some will buy only high tech stocks, others will buy only municipal bonds, etc) The companies attempt to obtain growth in the fund by growth in the value of the underlying stocks, but there's no guarantee of this. The advantage for most investors is that for a relatively small amount of money, they can participate in the ownership of many different companies and receive expert investment help. It's estimated that there are now over 18,000 mutual funds available for investors.

Pension—The most common use of this term is to describe a "Defined Benefit Retirement Plan." It's a type of retirement plan where the employee and employer both contribute to the retirement account. When the employee retires, he/she is promised a specific, defined amount of monthly payment for as long as they live.

Prenuptial Agreement—Is an legally binding agreement that two people about to be re-married enter into. It says that when one of the new partners dies, the assets that that new partner brought into the new marriage, would stay with the children from the first marriage, rather than go to the children of the new marriage.

Reverse Mortgage—Is the borrowing of money from an institution, using your home as collateral. It's a mortgage because the house is the collateral and the payments are determined like a mortgage: interest rate, value of the home, and length of time the owner is expected to live. The owner receives a monthly payment for as long as they live.

Required Minimum Distribution—Is an IRS rule that says at age 70 ½ a person must start taking money our of almost all retirement plans they own. (Roth IRAs are not included, for instance) The IRS has a specific formula for this distribution of money. Even if the owner doesn't spend the money, they must pay full income tax (state and federal) on the amount of money withdrawn. It's designed to try and empty the retirement accounts by the time the person dies.

Roll-over-Tax-Free—Is a process allowed by the IRS, where a person who has left employment can move their former retirement account (Like a 401(K), for instance) from one type of account to a Self-directed IRA without paying any taxes to move it.

Roth IRA—Is a special type of IRA in which after-tax money is put in, invested in mutual funds, usually, grows tax-deferred, and may be taken out tax-free. There are limits as to how much may be put into the Roth each year.

Russell 2000—Is an "index" of smaller companies who sell their stock to the public. The index tracks the price movements of a selected 2000 companies and records the "average" price movements of these types of stocks. Can be used as a benchmark to measure other mutual fund performance against.

Russell 1000—Is similar to the 2000 except this index tracks large companies' price movements.

Self-Directed IRA—Is an IRA that is "directed" by the investor. Meaning, the investor can pick and choose what investments to put into the IRA rather than another company limiting the investment choices as is usually the case with a 401(k), for instance. The Self-Directed IRA has the most flexibility and freedom of choice for the investor.

Tax-deferred vs. Tax-free—Tax-deferred means that income taxes are only deferred to a later date—eventually, they must be paid. Tax-free means that income taxes are never required to be paid.

Tax-Sheltered Annuities—Are retirement programs where employees put money into a retirement account, the money grows tax-deferred, and when taken out, is fully taxable. Investments inside these are usually mutual funds. They are sold and managed by insurance companies. Depending on a person' place of employment, these may be the only retirement accounts offered.

Uniform Transfer to Minors—Is a savings plan where a person can transfer ownership of an investment to a minor child. The adult owner remains the custodian of the money for the child until the child turns 18. At that time, the child obtains control of the money. The advantage is that the growth of the money is taxed at the child's tax rate. Once 529 College plans and Coverdell Savings plans became available, the popularity of these dropped.

Volatility—A term that refers to the natural ups and downs of any market. The stock market, bond market, real estate markets, all go up and down in price. This movement is known as volatility.

Variable Universal Life Insurance—Is a type of permanent insurance where the insured invests more than the premium amount into a variety of mutual funds. He/she has the potential for tax-deferred growth within the policy. The amount invested may be varied and the choices of investments may be changed. If the insured "borrows" the money out of the policy, it's a tax-free event.

Will—Is a "road map" written by a person to give instructions to others (usually family) on how to handle questions after death. Typically, these include the distribution of money and assets from the estate of the deceased to the beneficiaries.

Appendix

Additional information for quick reference. Usually, the internet is the easiest, mostly free, way to obtain more detailed information.

Online calculator for retirement income needs

    www.choosetosave.org

Life expectancy estimates—how long may you live?

    www.livingto100.com

How much can you spend in retirement? Also includes some Monte Carlo modeling. This web site has a huge amount of additional information about many financial subjects also

    www.troweprice.com

Monte Carlo modeling and probabilities—an explanation of the academic foundations

    www.drsamsavage.com

Mutual fund rankings and analysis. They also include some retirement planning advice

    www.Morningstar.com

Saving for retirement—computer models. (Costs a fee to join)

    www.financialengines.com

Retirement planning and Monte Carlo analysis. This huge website includes a variety of financial tools for many different questions

    www.fidelity.com

Retirement planning. Another huge website for broad financial advice

    www.vanguard.com

List of Certified Financial Planners. May help you choose where to begin looking for a counselor to help you with retirement questions

www.cfpboard.org

Buying US Treasury bills. Enables you to buy directly

www.treasurydirect.gov

IRA help from an expert. Ed Slott has written an excellent, thorough book on the "ins and outs" of IRA's.

www.irahelp.com

Social Security questions answered

www.socialsecurity.gov

Medicare questions answered

www.medicare.gov

Search for temporary health care coverage after you quit or retire

www.healthinsurance.com

Calculator to figure out the monthly income to be obtained from an Immediate Annuity

www.immediateannuities.com

Annuity information

www.annuityinsights.com

www.annuityadvantage.com

Information about Reverse Mortgages from the Financial Freedom Senior Funding Corp.

www.financialfreedom.com

Long Term Care insurance group policy information

www.aarp.org

www.metlife.com/aarp

www.gltc.Jhancock.com

Social Security official website

www.ssa.gov

Bibliography

These are books recommended for further information on a variety of the subjects discussed in this book.

Stocks for the Long Run, Jeremy Siegel, McGraw-Hill, New York, 1998 (Dr. Siegel makes a classic, solid case for investing in the stock market)

The Future for Investors, Jeremy Siegel, Crown Business Books, New York, 2005

Devil Take the Hindmost, Edward Chancellor, Penguin Putnam, Inc., New York, 2000 (A well written history of market "bubbles" and lessons about them for today)

The New Rules of Retirement, Robert C. Carlson, John Wiley & Sons, Inc., New Jersey, 2005 (Addresses many of the problems people face in retirement with strategies to avoid)

Missed Fortune 101, Douglas R. Andrew, Warner Business Books, New York, 2005 (Unique ways to make better use of your home equity and reduce taxes)

The Savage Number, Terry Savage, John Wiley & Sons, Inc., New Jersey, 2005 (A review of many retirement issues with solutions)

The 7 Habits of Highly Effective People, Stephen R. Covey, Simon and Schuster, New York, 1989 (The title says it all)

Create Your Own Future, Brian Tracy, John Wiley & Sons, Inc. New Jersey, 2002 (The advantages of attitude, planning, and dreaming for your goals)

Play to Win! Larry Wilson, Bard Press, Austin, 1998 (How to identify negative factors in your life and what to do to change to positive ones)

The Road Less Traveled, M. Scott Peck, Simon and Schuster, New York, 1978 (The "bible" of self-help books: warns us that change is inevitable but, ultimately, freeing)

The Retirement Savings Time Bomb, Ed Slott, Penquin Books, New York, 2003 (An excellent, thorough study of IRAs and what's the best strategy for using them)

Simple Wealth, Inevitable Wealth, Nick Murray, Nick Murray Company, Inc, Mattitick, NY 1999 (A plan for learning about your money, saving, and investing that leads to success)

Unlimited Power, Anthony Robbins, Simon and Schuster, New York, 1986 (Another self-help book about attitude, modeling, and goal setting that can enable you to do things you couldn't imagine before)

An Empire of Wealth, John Steele Gordon, HarperCollins, New York, 2004 (Economic history of the U.S.—but—told in a journalistic, interesting way)

The Roaring 2000s: Building the wealth and life style you desire in the greatest boom in history. Harry S. Dent, Simon and Schuster, New York, 1998 (Reasons why the stock market is poised to make huge gains in the years ahead)

The Complete Idiot's Guide to Social Security, Lita Epstein, Alpha Books, Indianapolis, Indiana, 2002 (Don't let the title put you off. It is an easy, thorough guide to the maze of Social Security)

Winning the Loser's Game, Charles D. Ellis, McGraw-Hill, New York, 2002 (A concise guide to asset allocation and an investor's ability to be patient and wait for inevitable growth)

The Number, Lee Eisenberg, Free Press, New York, 2006 (An engaging read about the psychology behind deciding to quit)

Index